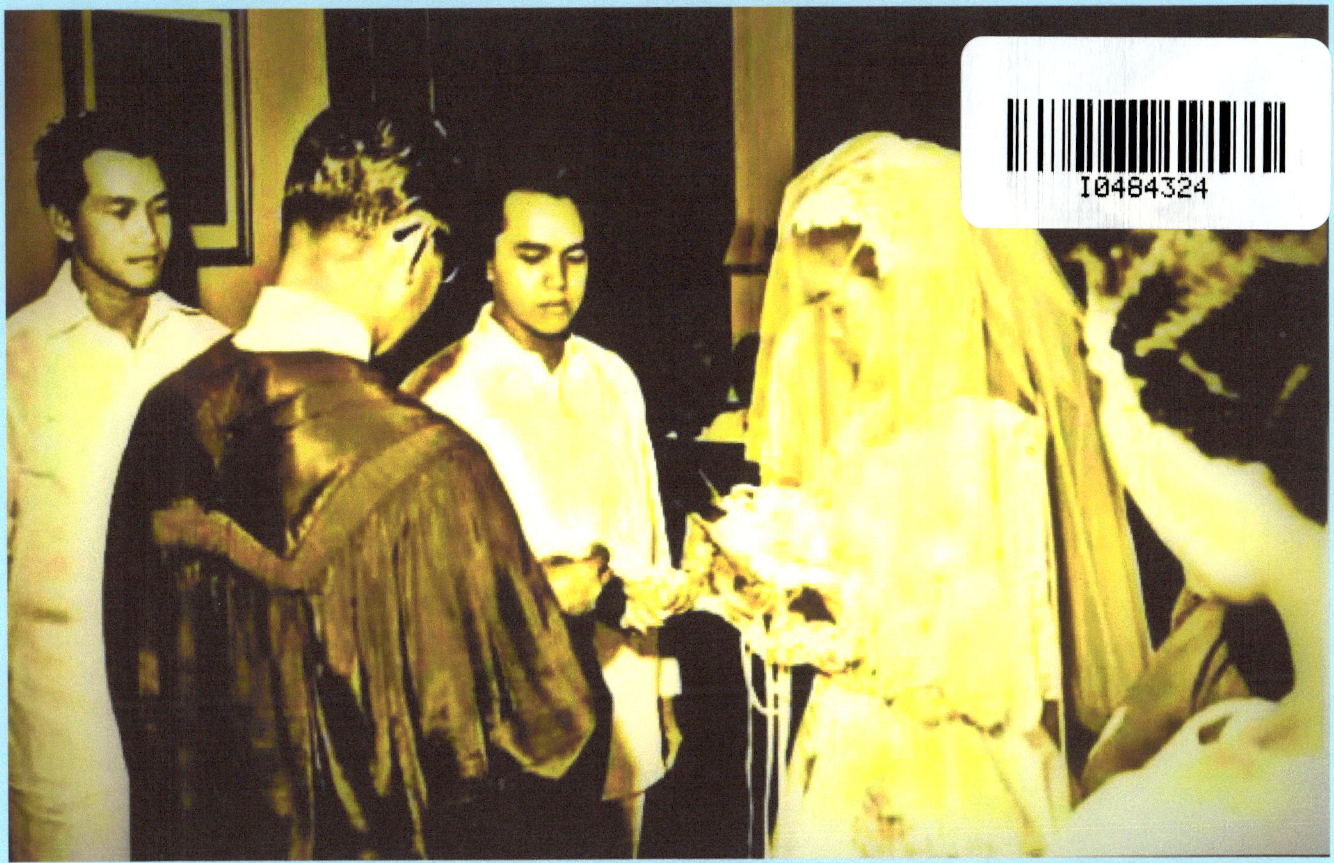

April 4, 1959 - Job & Cora Elizes Wedding at Ellinwood-Malate Church. L-R: Atty.Arte Guerrero (vice) Charles Hollmann, as Ninong + Rev. Pastor David Raymundo + Job (Groom) + Corazon (Bride) + Ruth Remorca, bridesmaid.

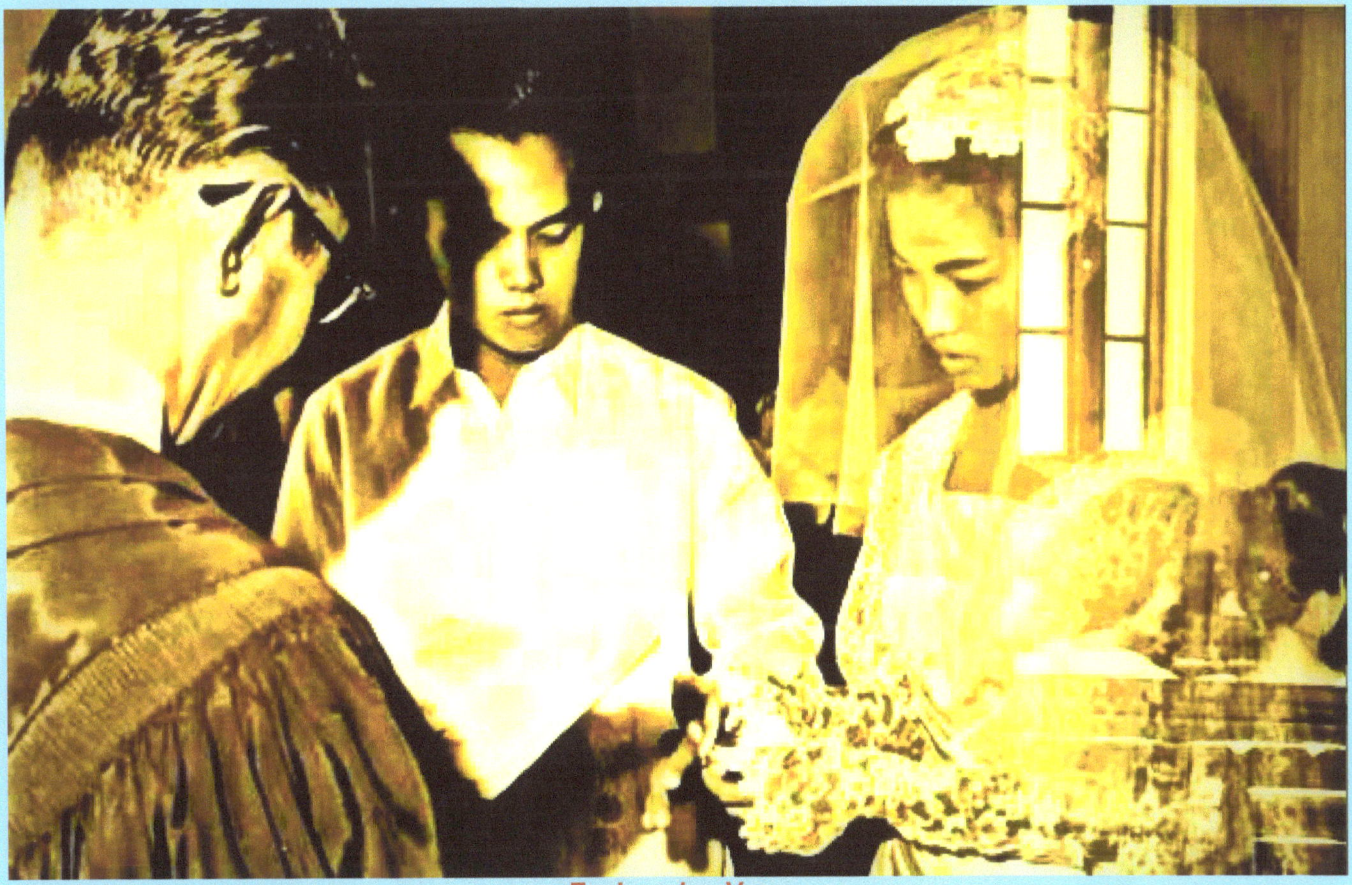

Exchanging Vows

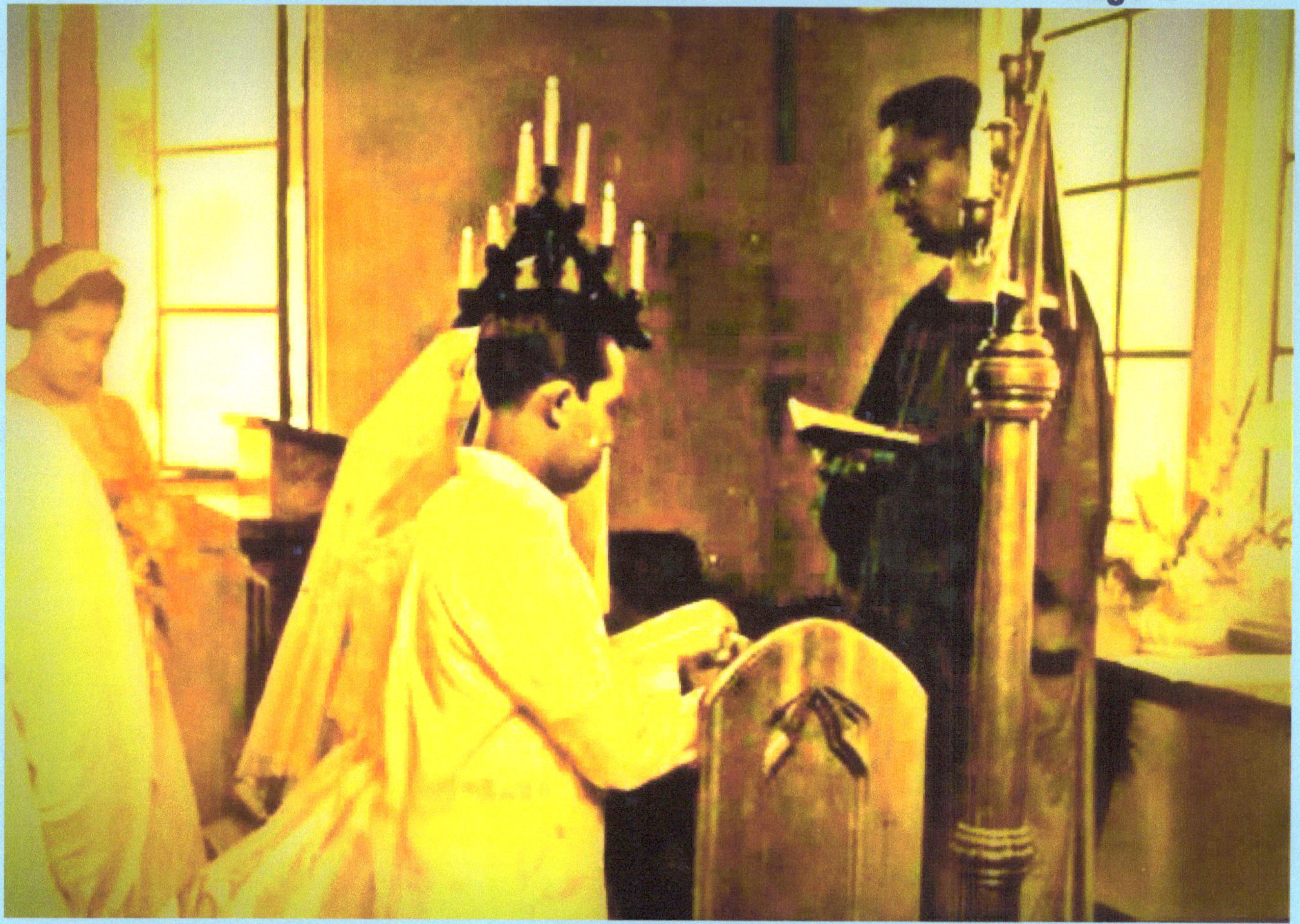

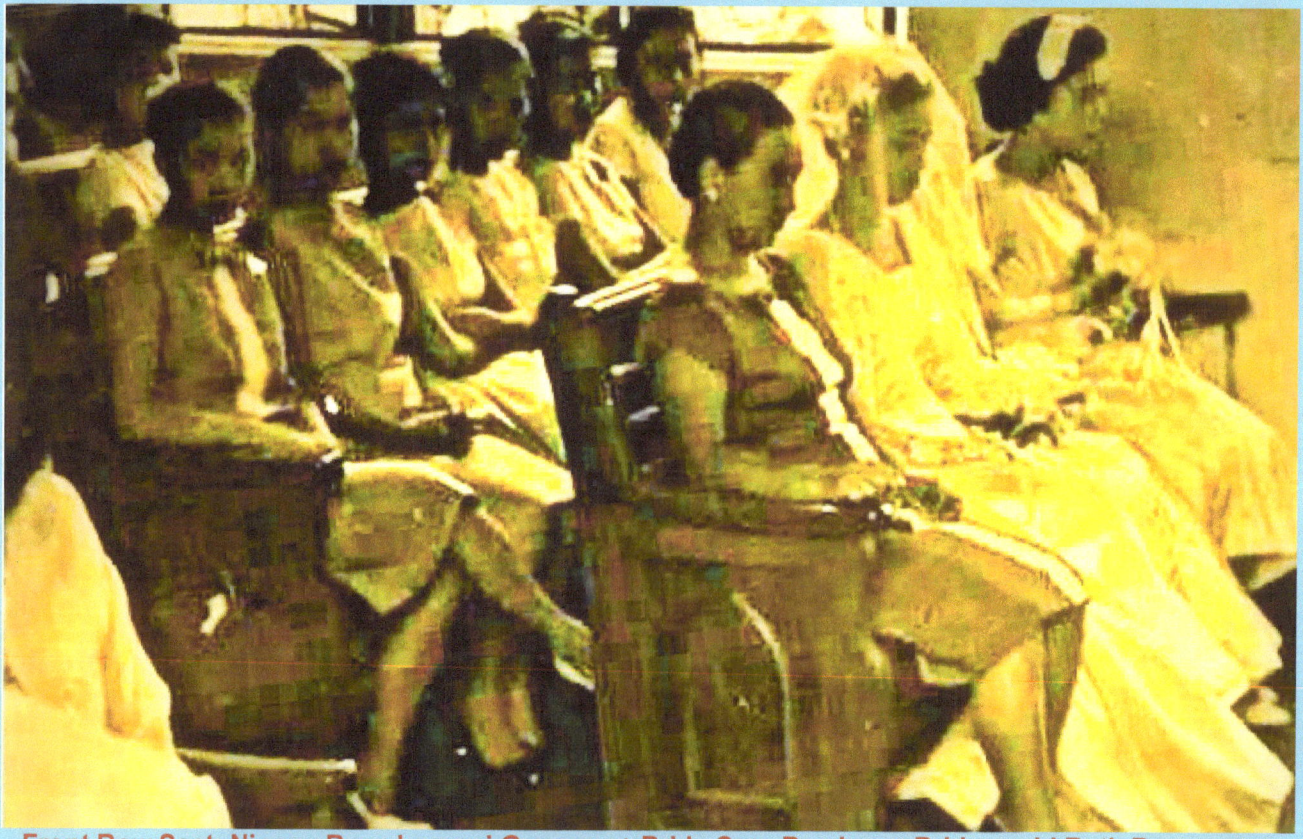

Pastoral Prayer

Front Row Seat: Ninang Rosa Legaspi Guerrero + Bride Cora Ramirez + Bridesmaid Ruth Remora + +
2nd Row Seat: Hilda Elizes + Friends-Guests

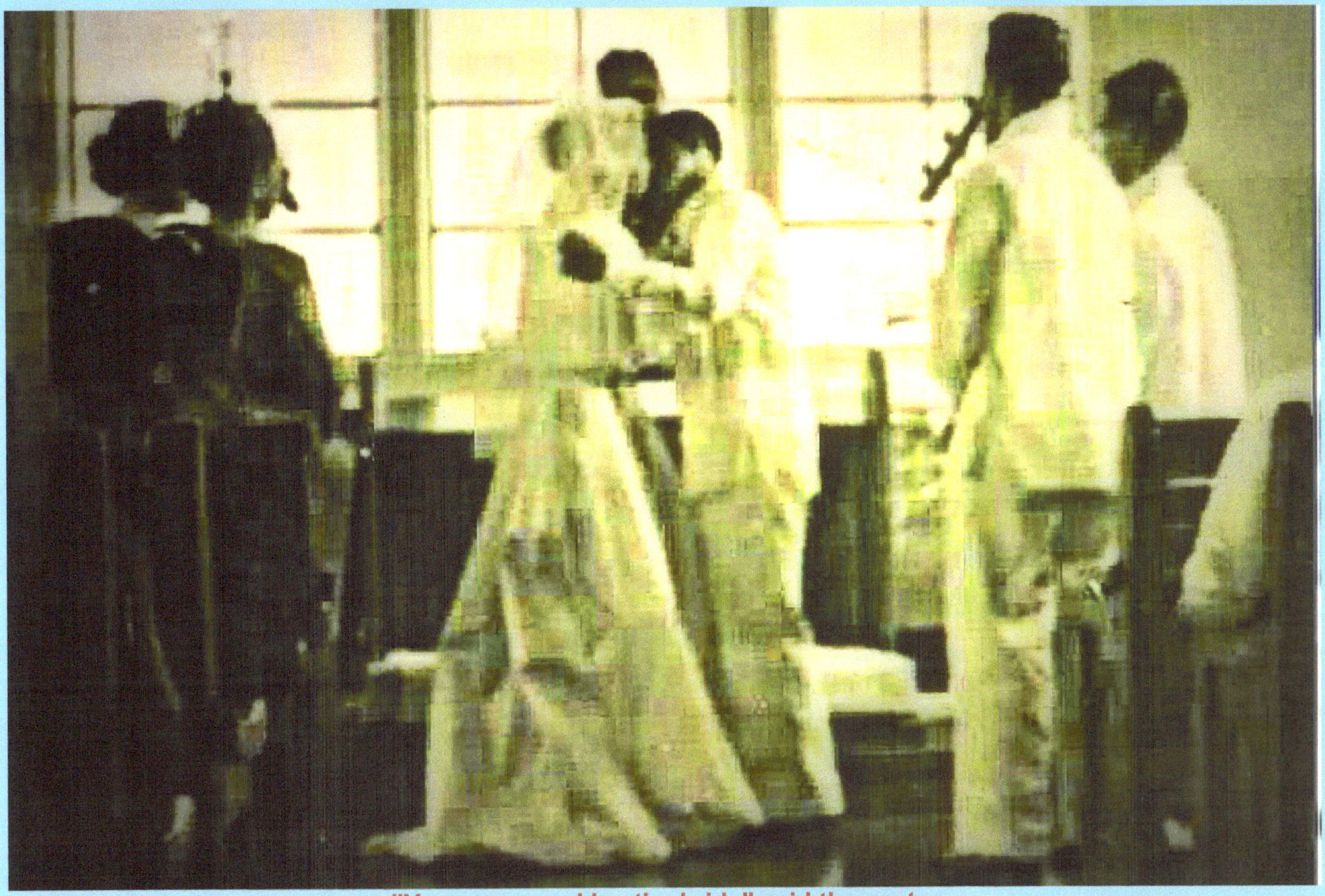

"You may now kiss the bride" said the pastor

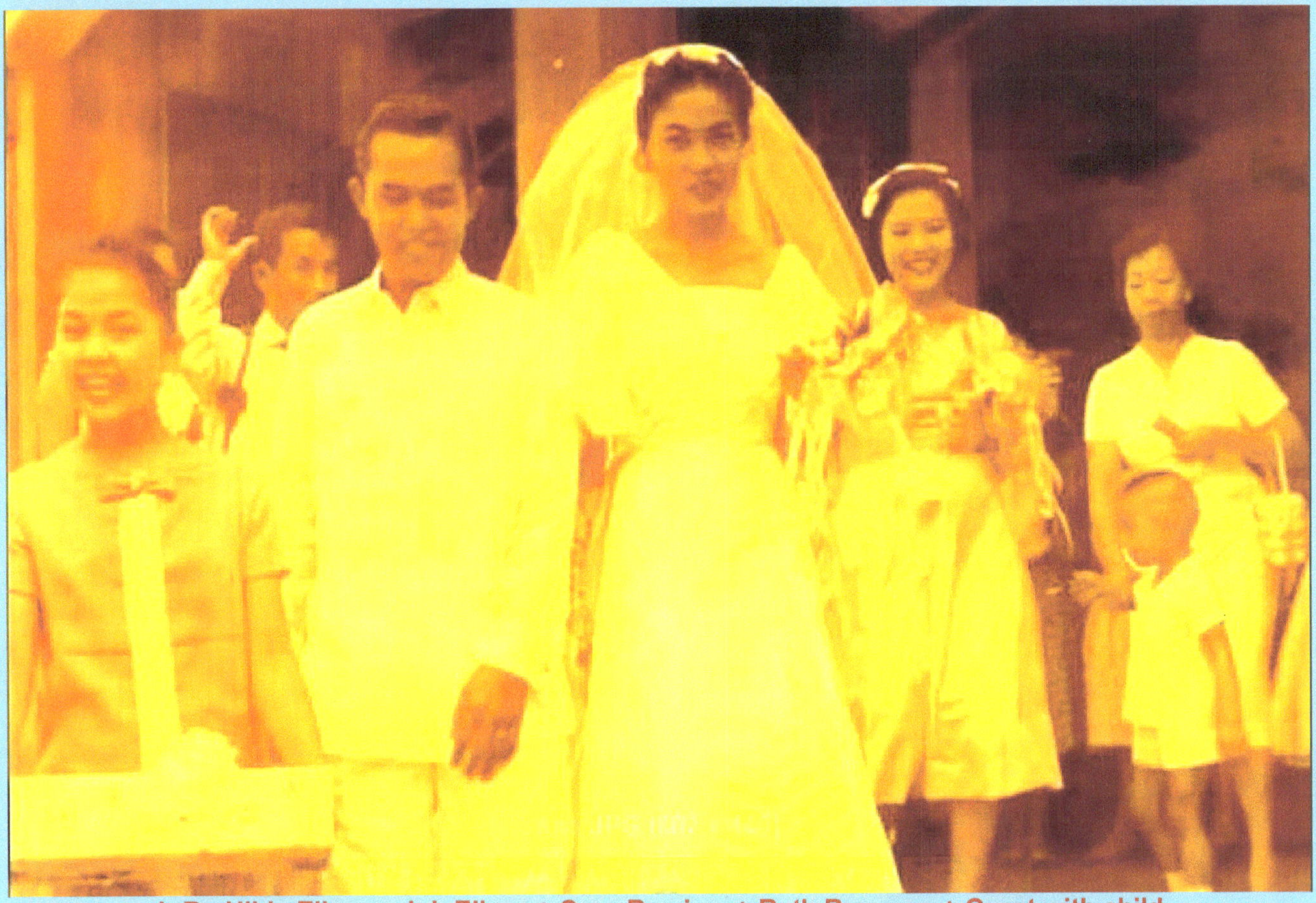

L-R: Hilda Elizes + Job Elizes + Cora Ramirez + Ruth Remorca + Guest with child

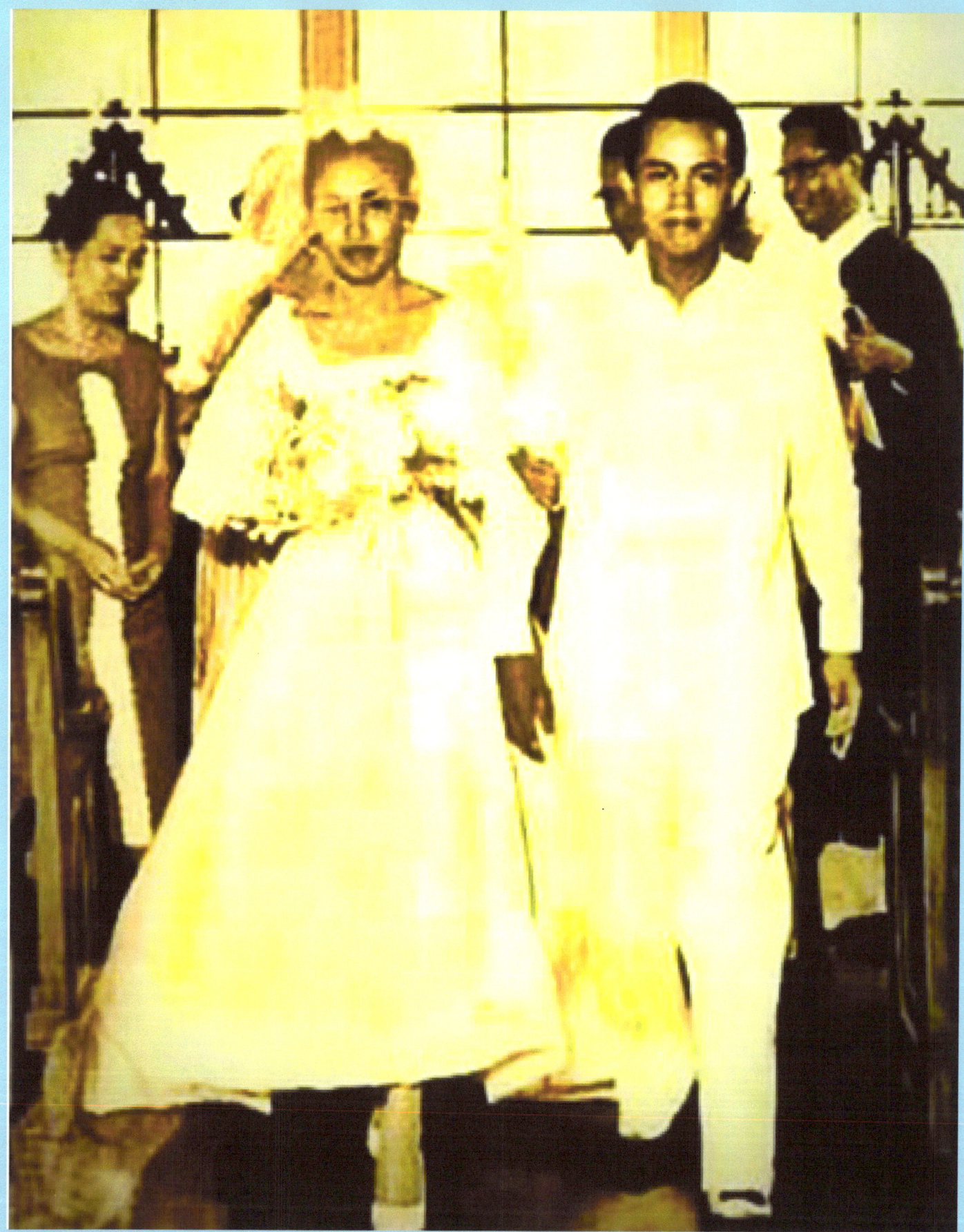

Recessional March

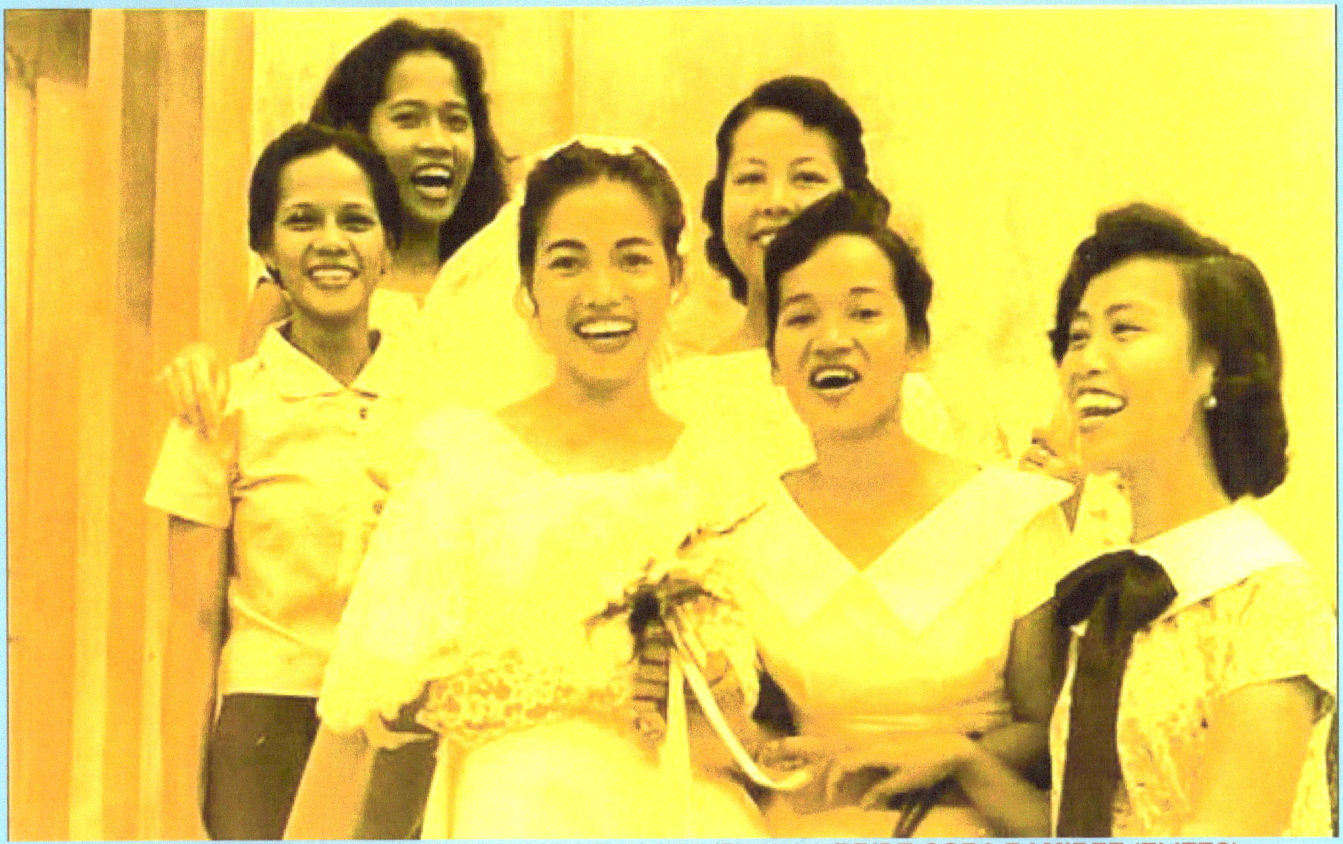

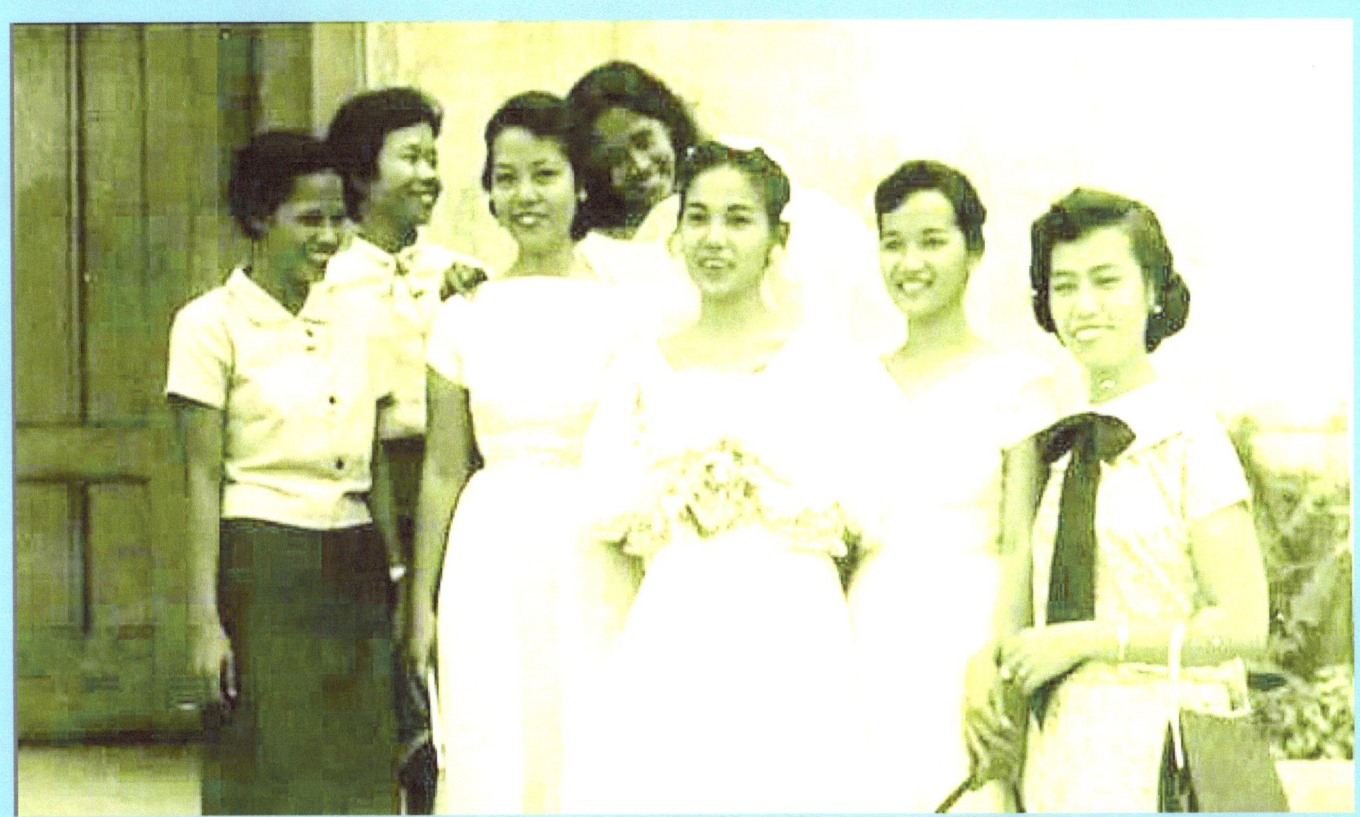

April 4, 1059: L-R: Ine Landasan + Nora Postrero (Boger) + BRIDE CORA RAMIREZ (ELIZES) +
Luzonica Majam (Bautista) + Tita Romana + Evelyn Majam (Llamas)

L-R: Ine Landasan + Friend + Luzonica Majam (Bautista) + Nora Postrero (Boger) +
CORA RAMIREZ (ELIZES) + Tita Romana + Evelyn Majam (Llamas)

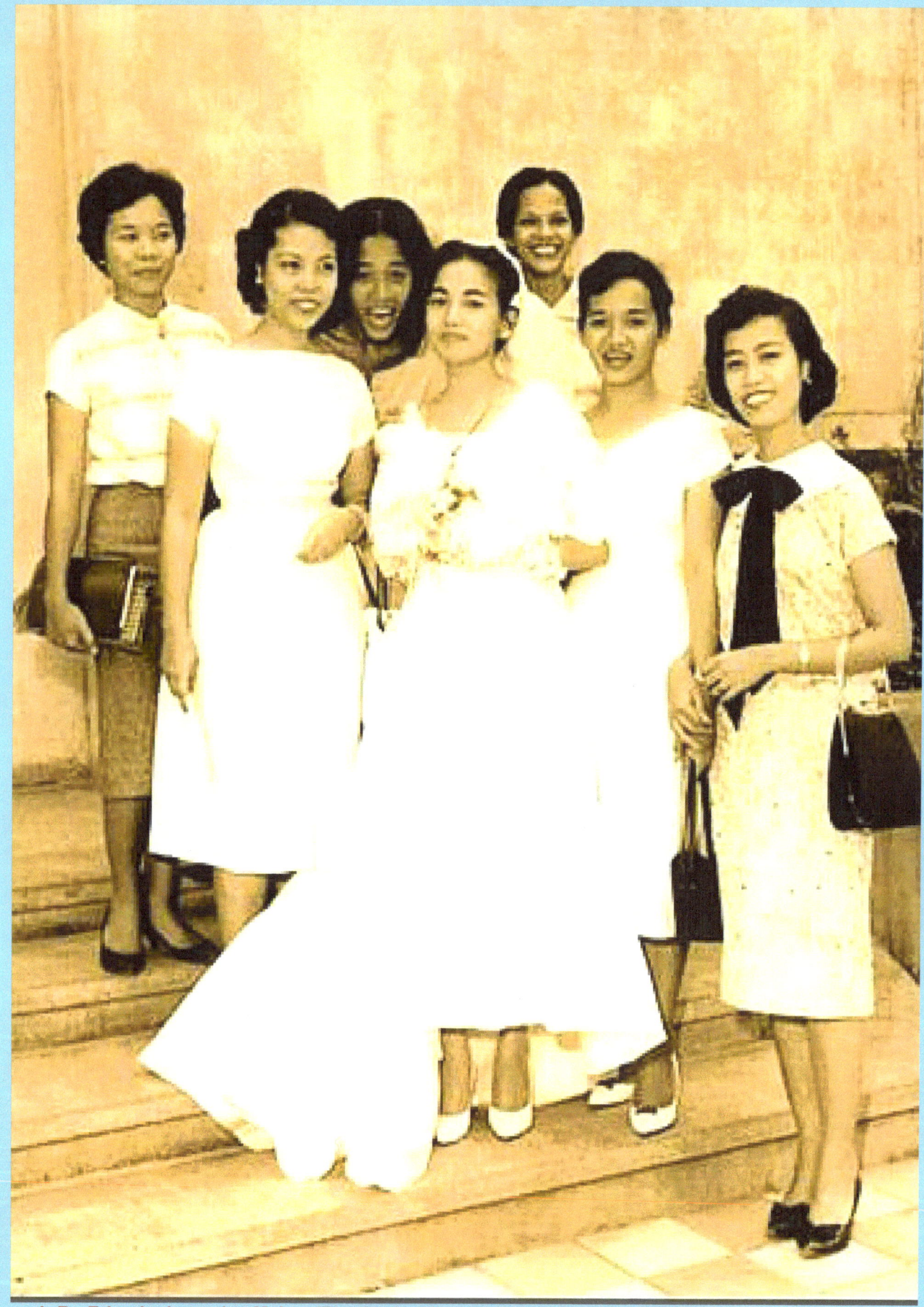

L-R: Friend + Luzonica Majam (Bautista) + Nora Postrero (Boger) + CORA RAMIREZ (ELIZES) +
Friend + Tita Romana + Evelyn Majam (Llamas) + Ine Landasan (at back)

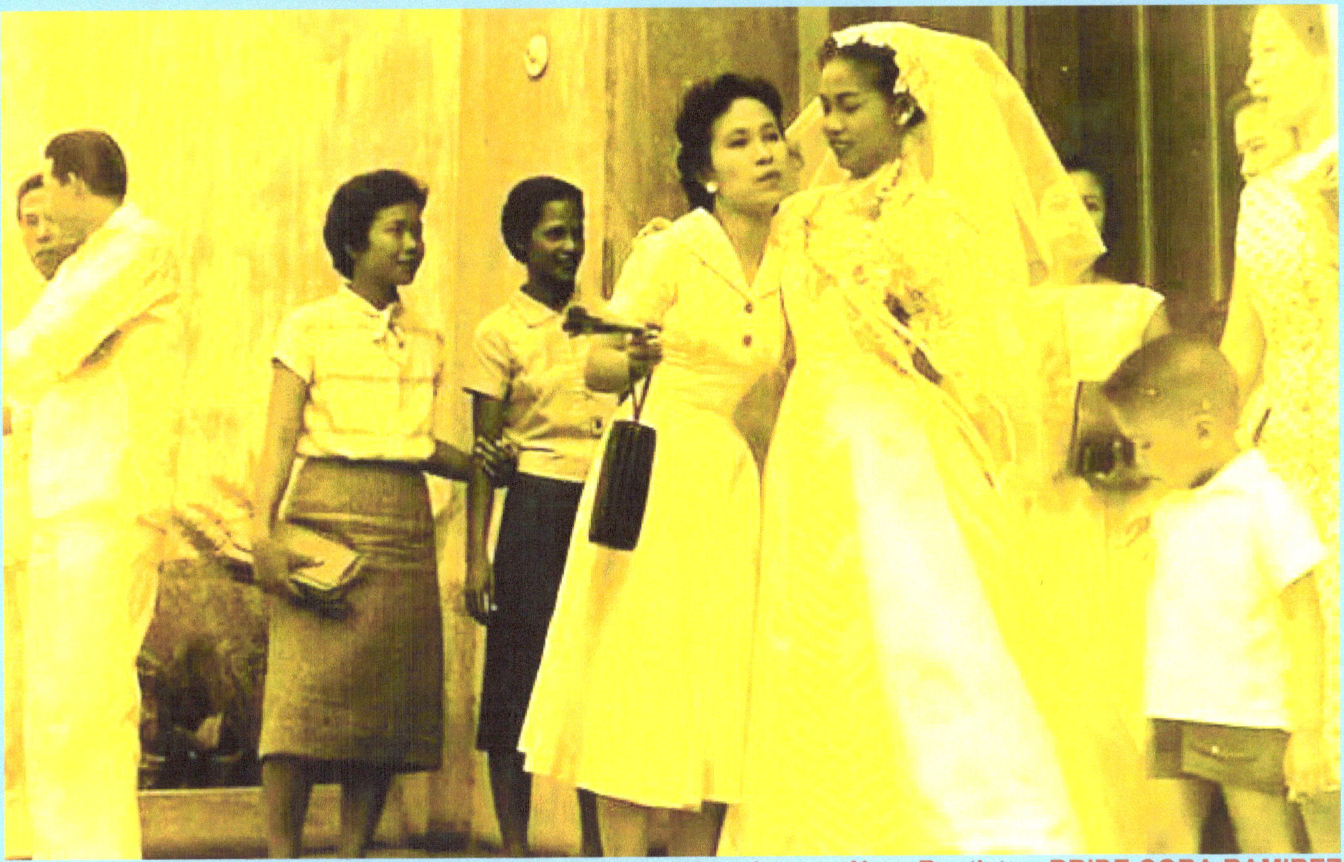

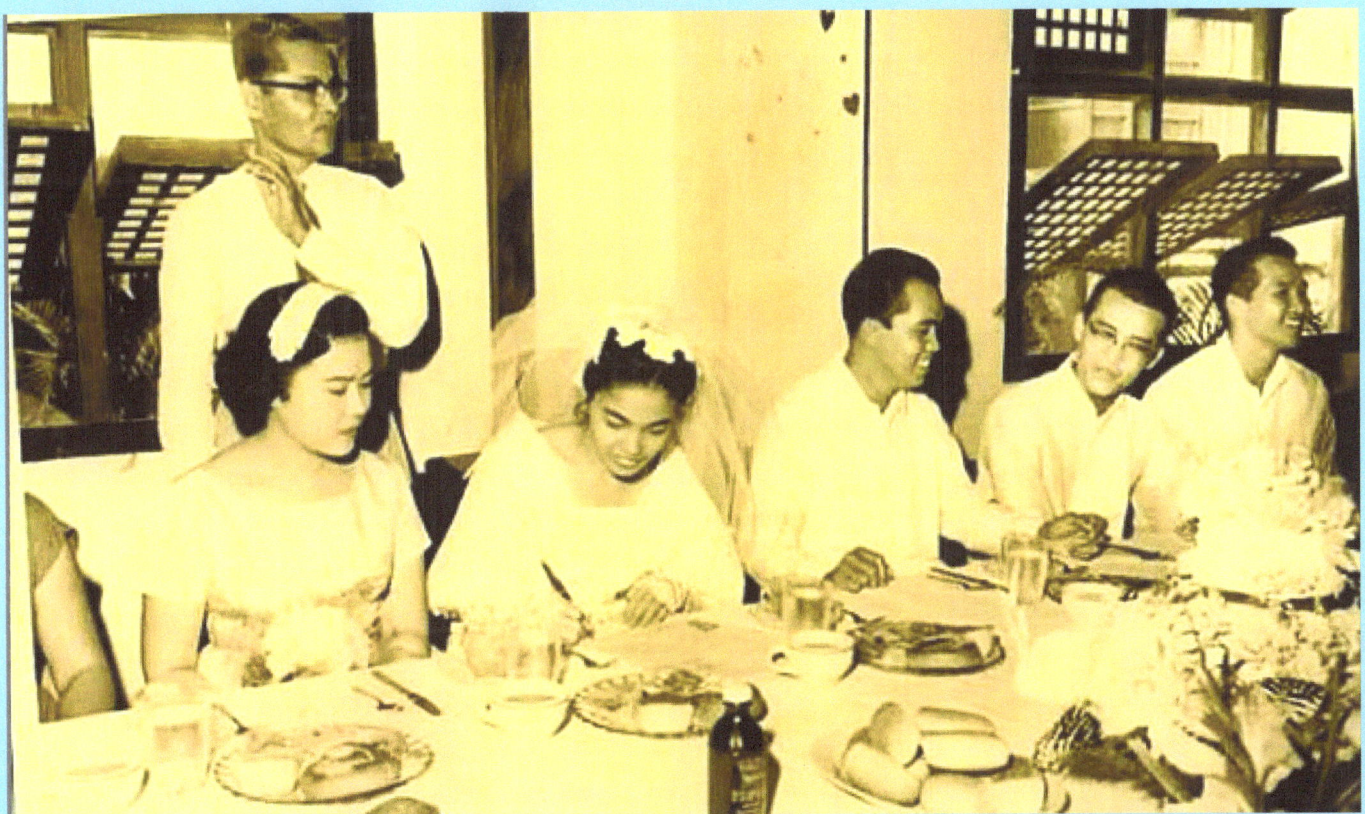

L-R: Arsenio Ferrer + Arte Guerrero + Lady guest + Ine Landasan + Necy Bautista + BRIDE CORA RAMIREZ + Lady guest at back + Cousin Ely Remorca + Young Noel Ferrer

L-R: Standing: Rev. Pastor David Raymundo + + Seated: Bridesmaid Ruth Remorca (Mercado) + BRIDE CORA RAMIREZ + GROOM JOB ELIZES JR + Best Man Gene Guerrero + Ninong Arte Guerrero (in behalf of Charles Hollmann)

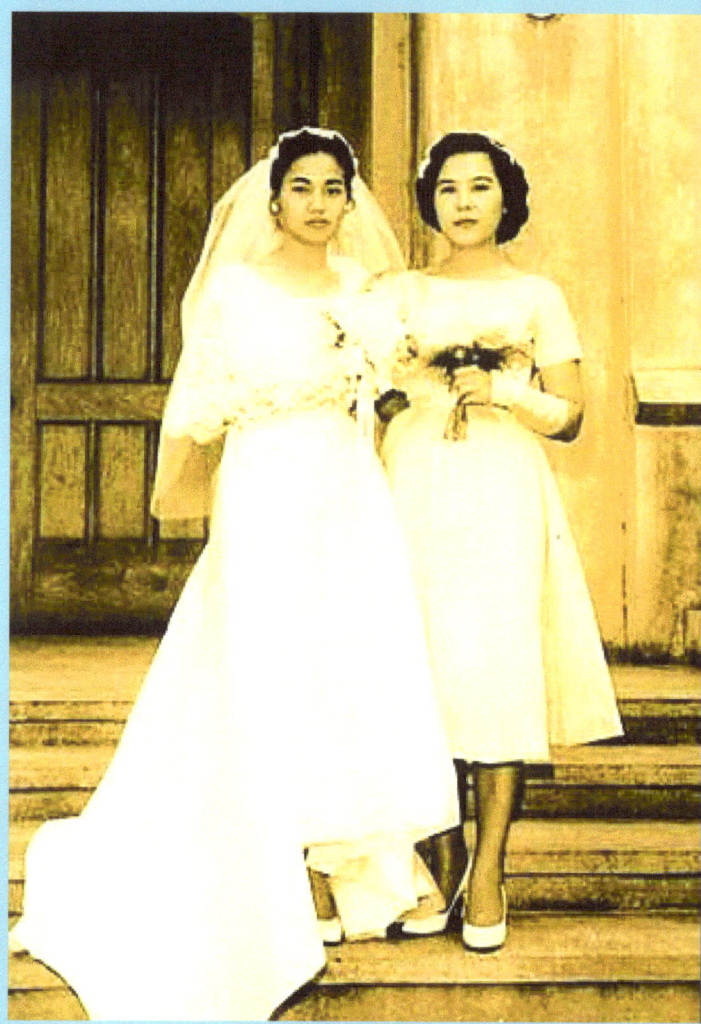

Cousins Cora Ramirez and Ruth Remorca

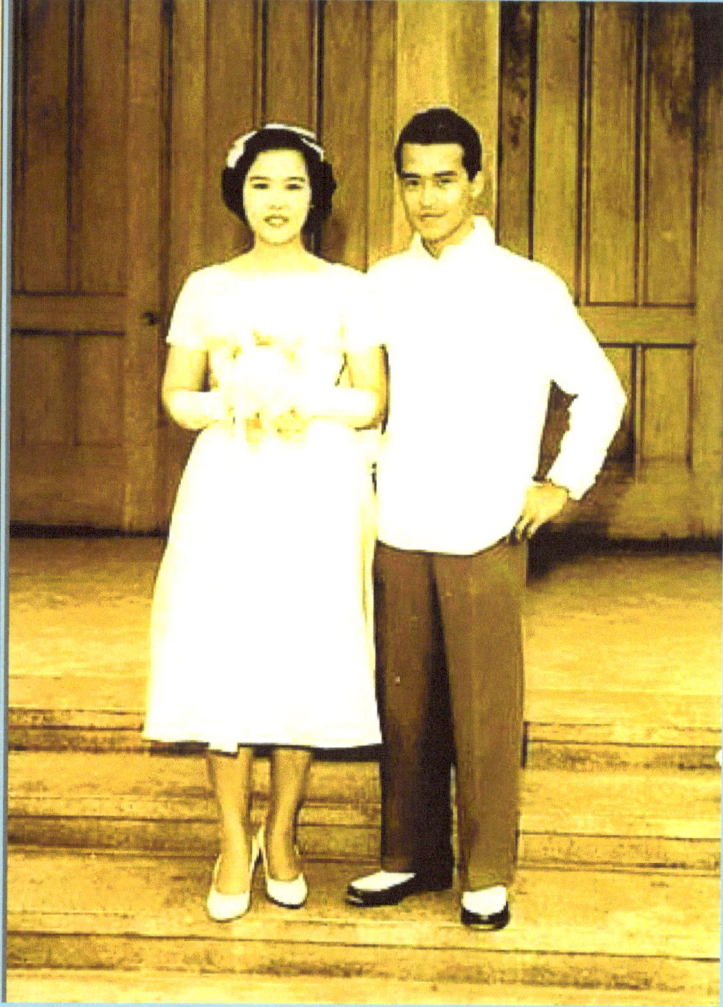

Bridesmaid & Bestman: Ruth Remorca & Gene Guerrero

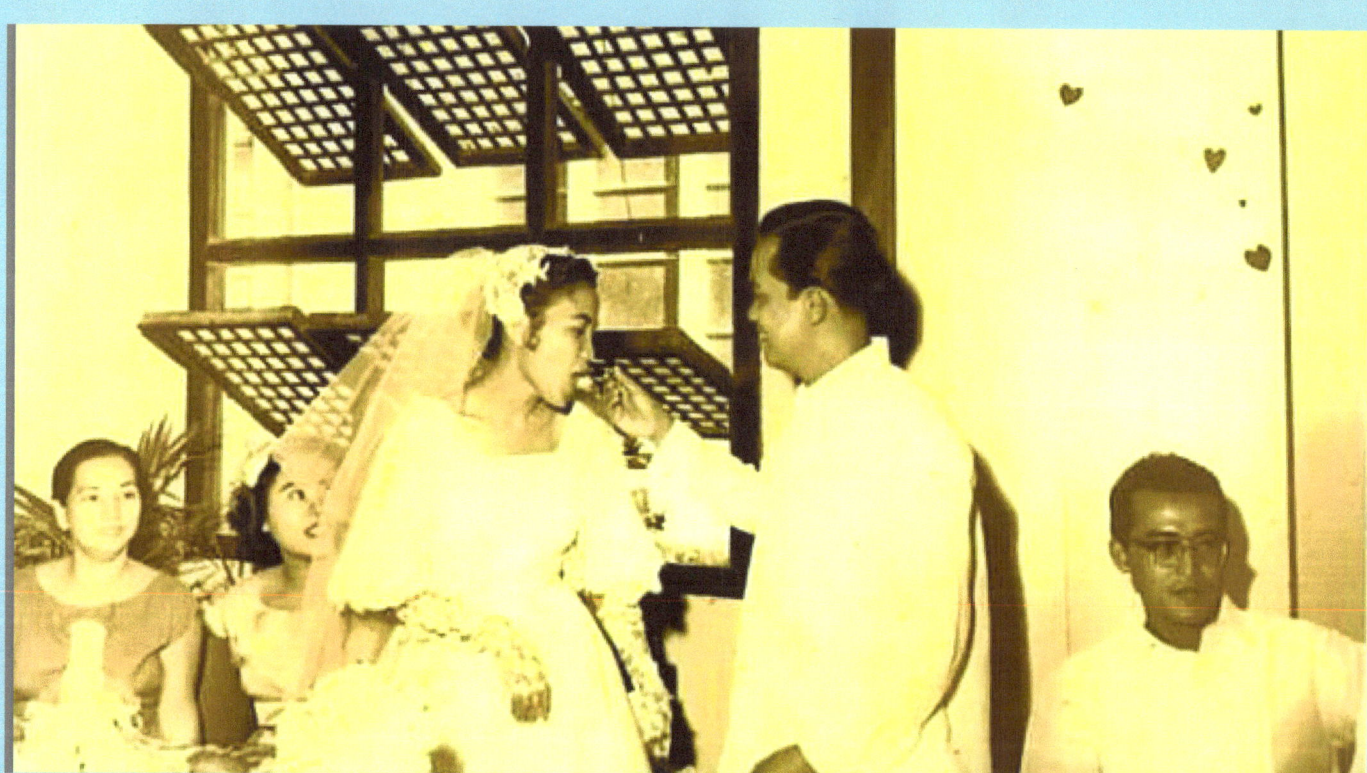

L-R: Ninang Rosing Guerrero + Bridesmaid Ruth Remorca + BRIDE & GROOM CORA & JOB + Bestman Gene Guerrero

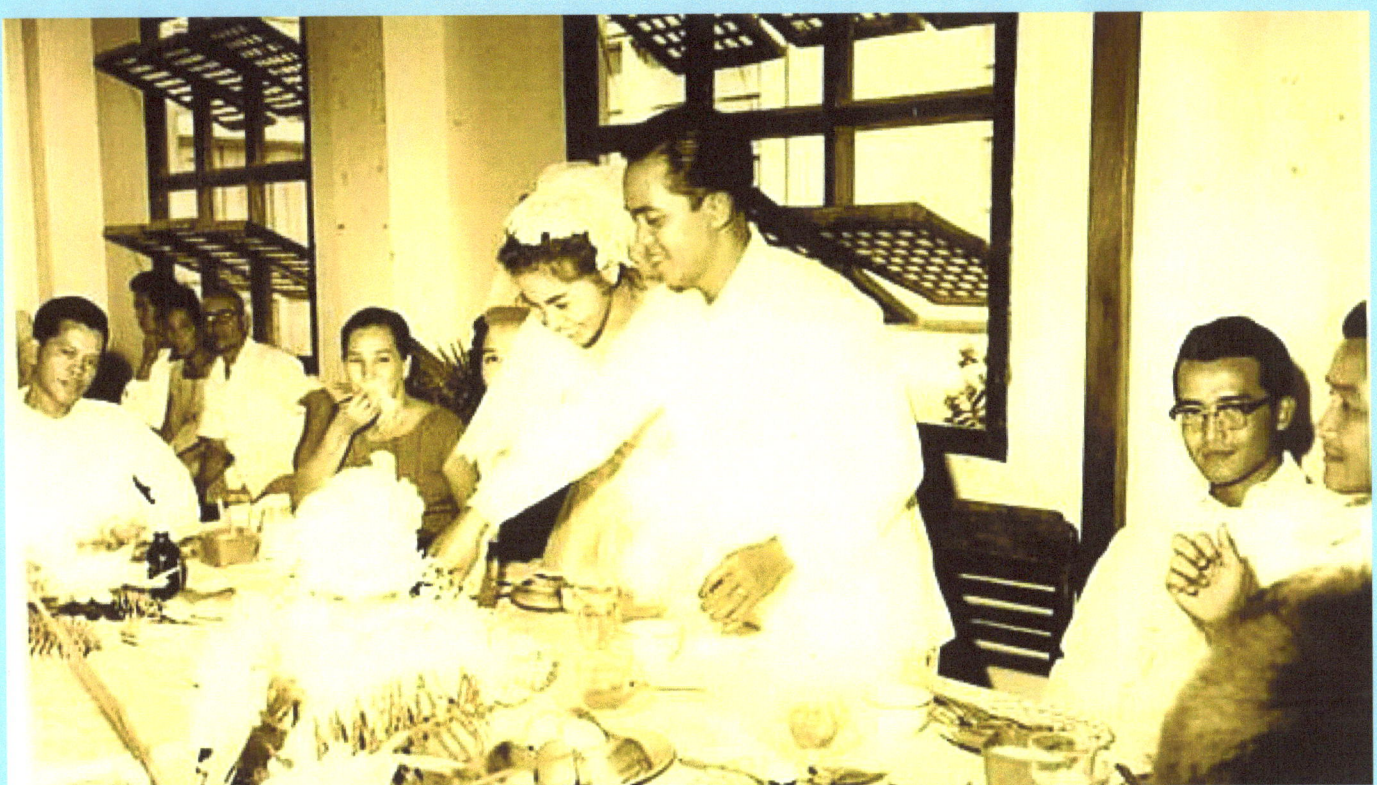

L-R: Tio Joaquin Bautista + Ninang Tia Rosing Guerrero + Ruthie Remorca (partly) +
BRIDE & GROOM CORA & JOB + Bestman Tio Gene Guerrero + Ninong Tio Arte Guerrero

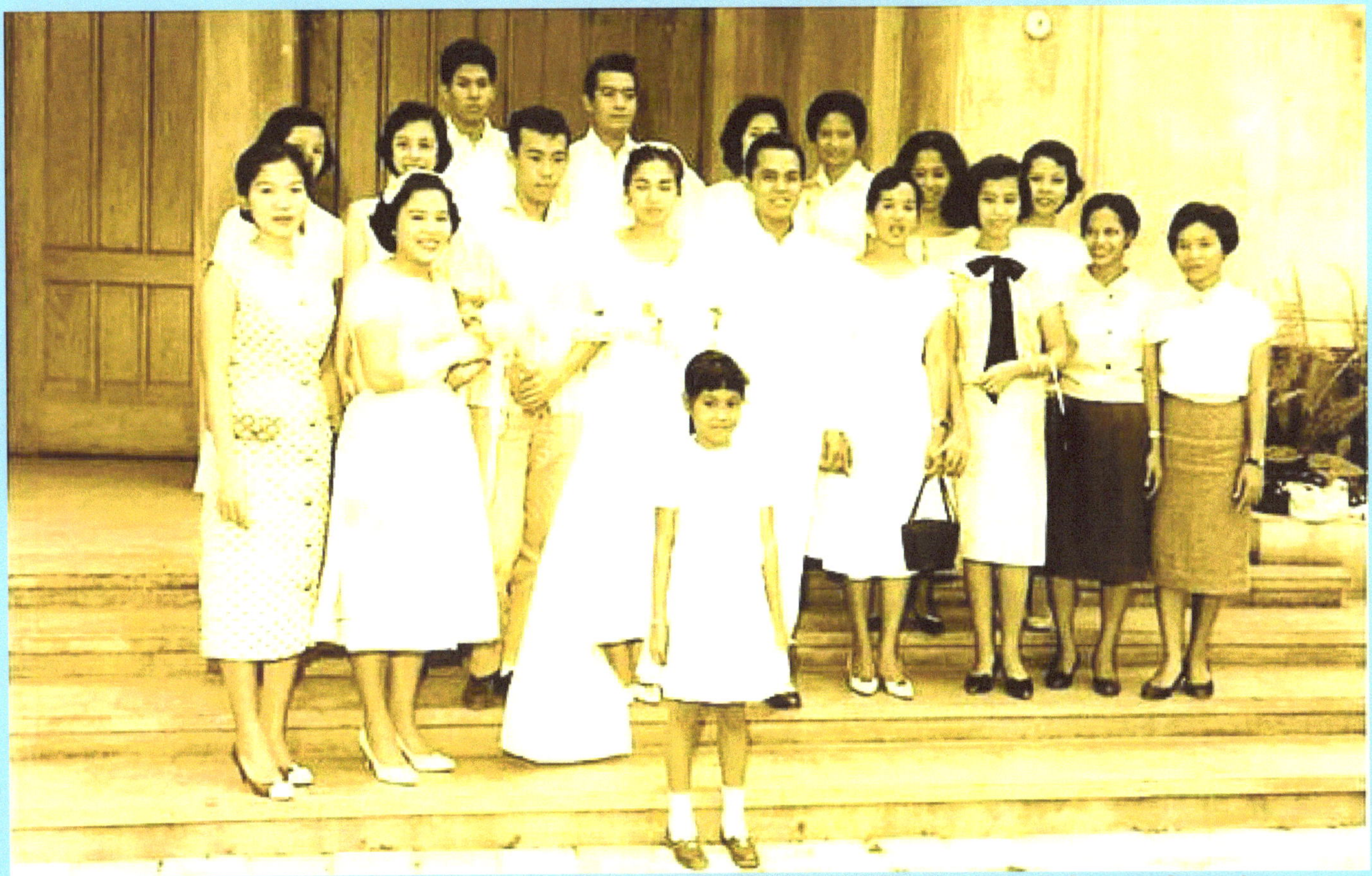

Shown: Front: Emma Sapinoso + + 1st Row: Ely Remorca + Ruthie Remorca + George Gonzales +
BRIDE CORA +GROOM JOB + Tita Romana + Evelyn Majam + Ine Landasan + Friend + + Back Row: Friend +
Felicing Remorca ++ Mel Lasam + Joe DeHitta + Friend + Norma Tiongson + Nora Postrero + Zony Majam

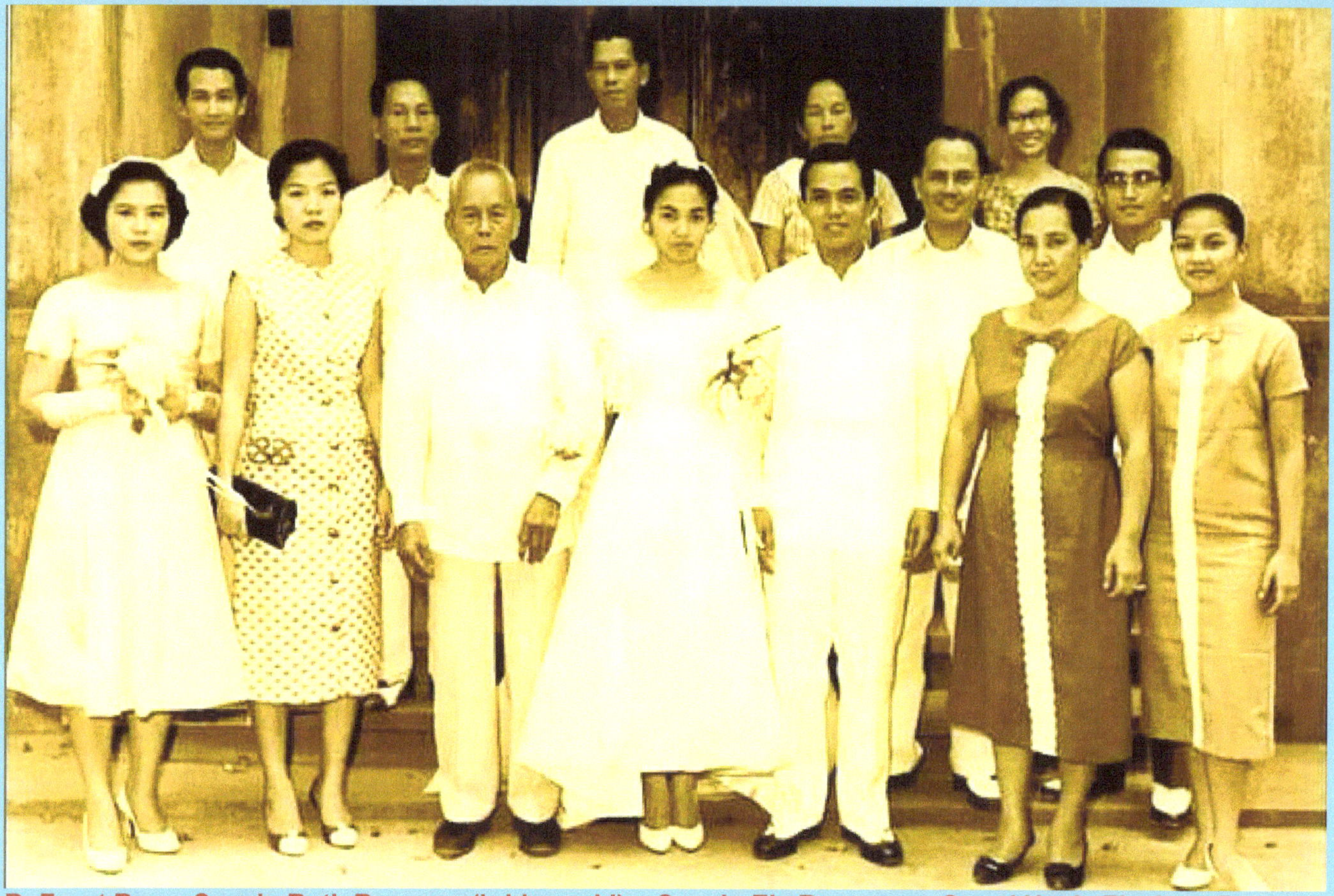

L-R: Front Row: Cousin Ruth Remorca (bridesmaid) + Cousin Ely Remorca + Grand Uncle Flaviano Remorca + BRIDE & GROOM (CORA RAMIREZ AND JOB ELIZES JR) + Ninang Tia Rosing Guerrero + sister Hilda Elizes + Back Row: Ninong Tio Arte Guerrero (in behalf of Charles Hollmann) + Uncle Mr. Sapinoso + Joaquin Bautista + Nanay Lucila Bautista Ramirez + Daddy Job Elizes Sr. + Ms. Fidela Gonzales + Bestman Tio Gene Guerrero

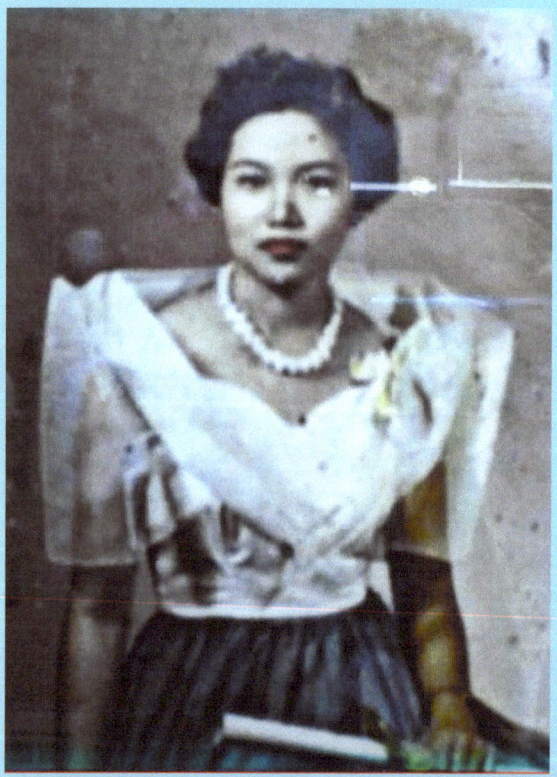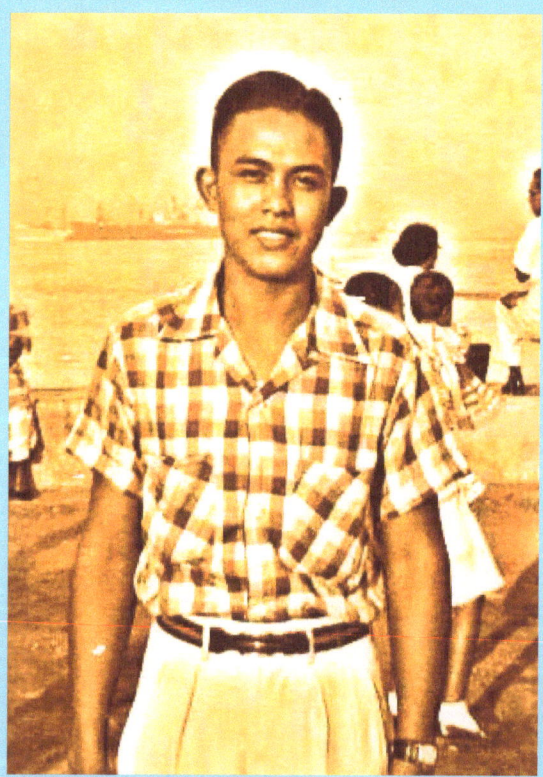

L-R: 1955, Cora Graduation at Harris Memorial College + + 1953: Job's 2nd Yr at Mapua

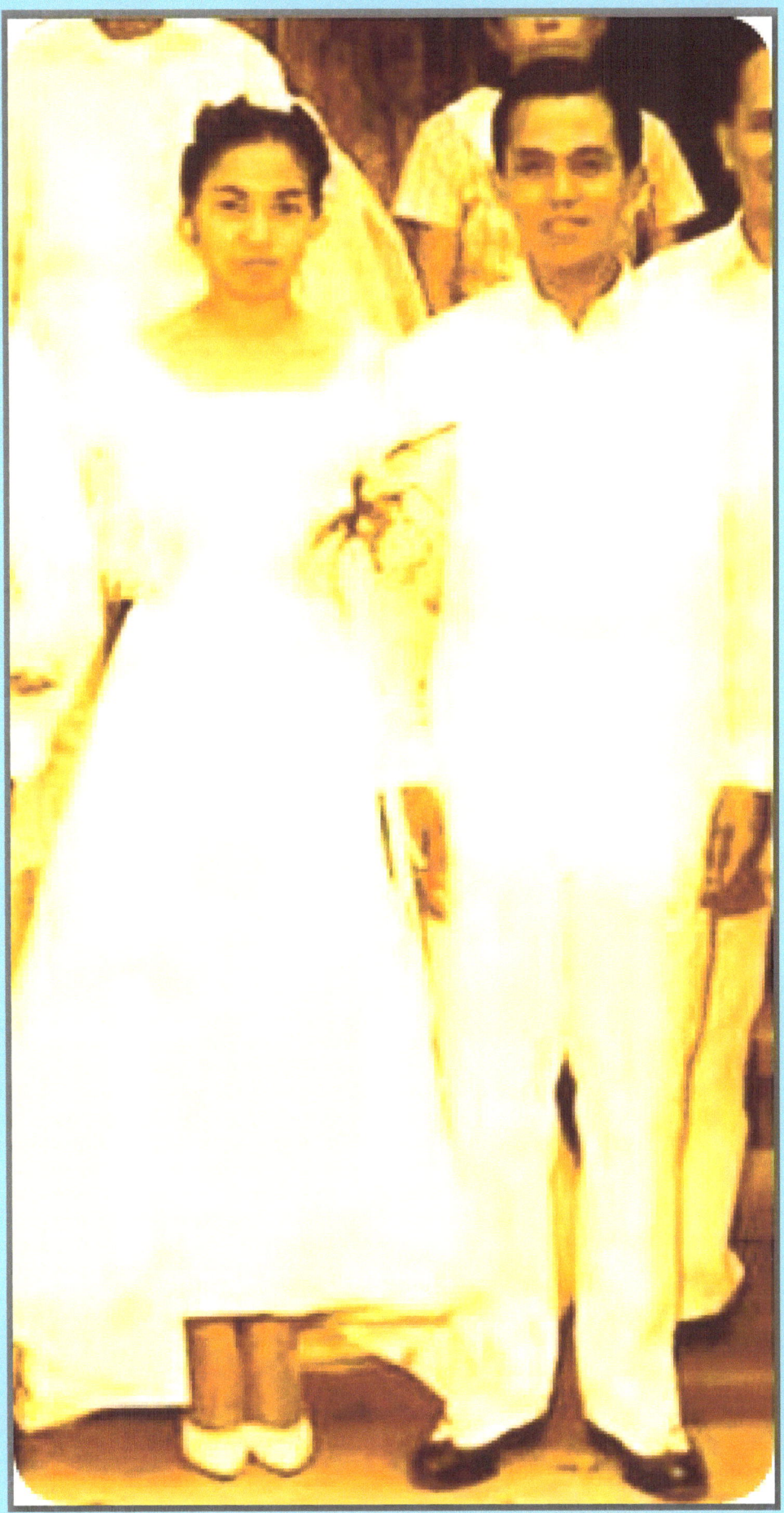

April 4, 1959 - Wedding of Job Elizes & Cora Ramirez

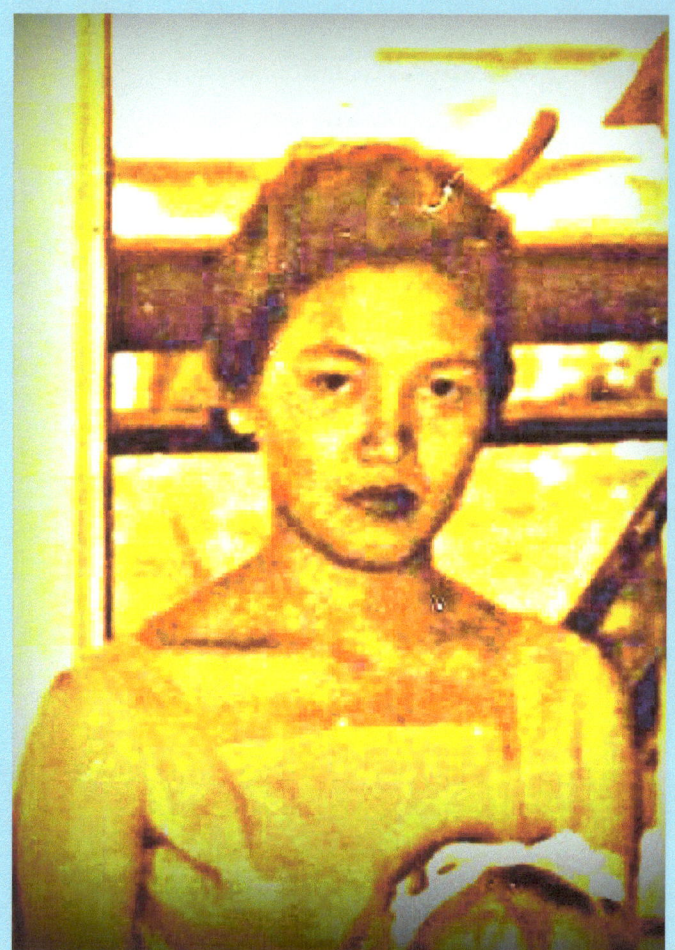

Circa 1956: Cora at 20

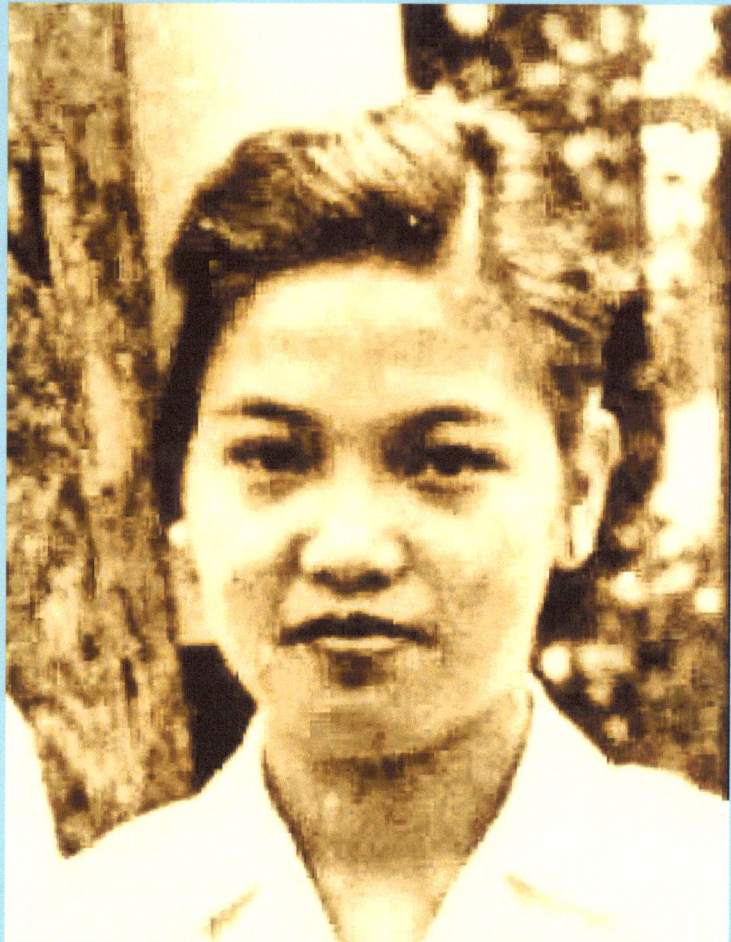

Circa 1955: Cora at 19

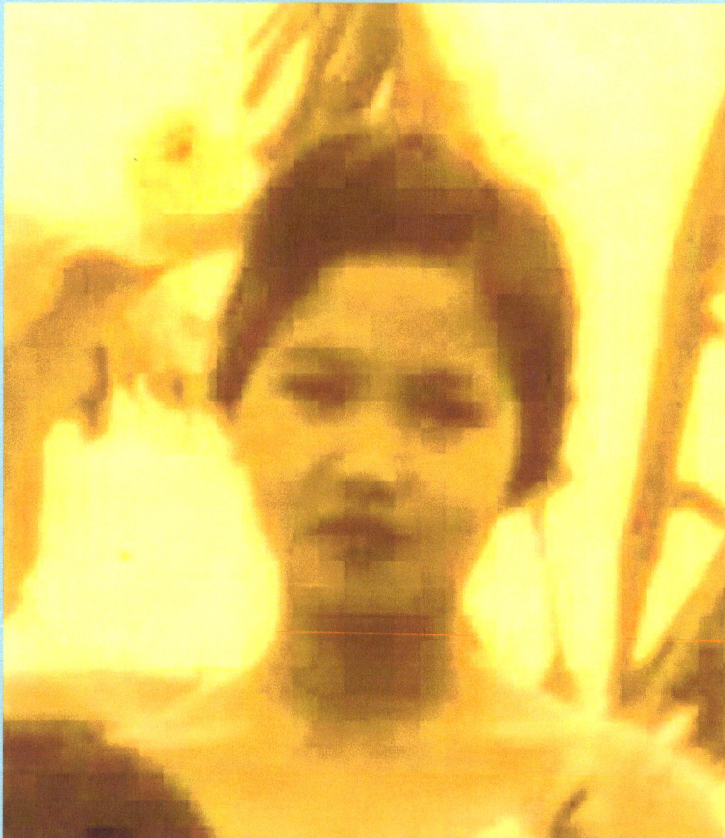

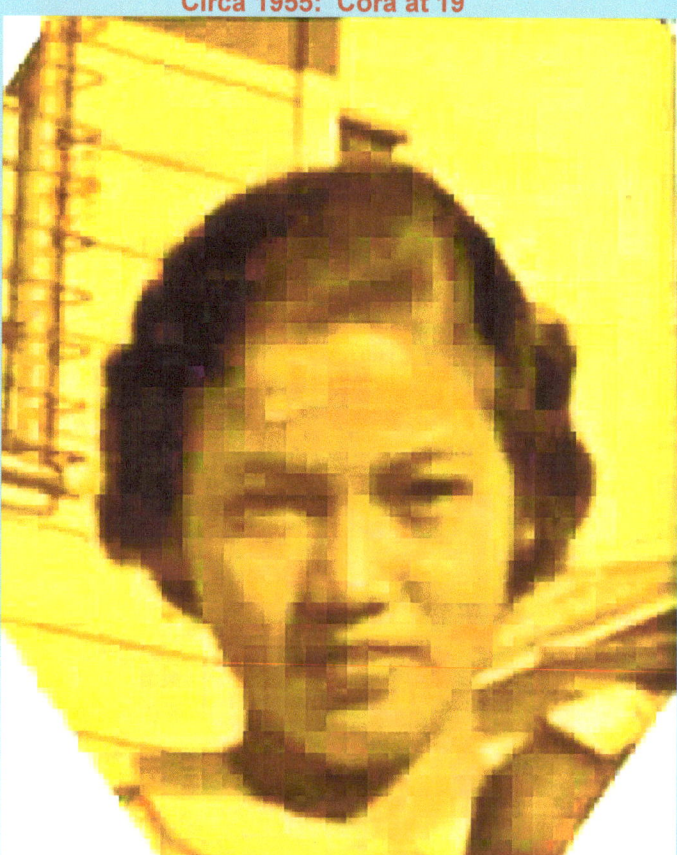

Circa 1956: Cora at 20

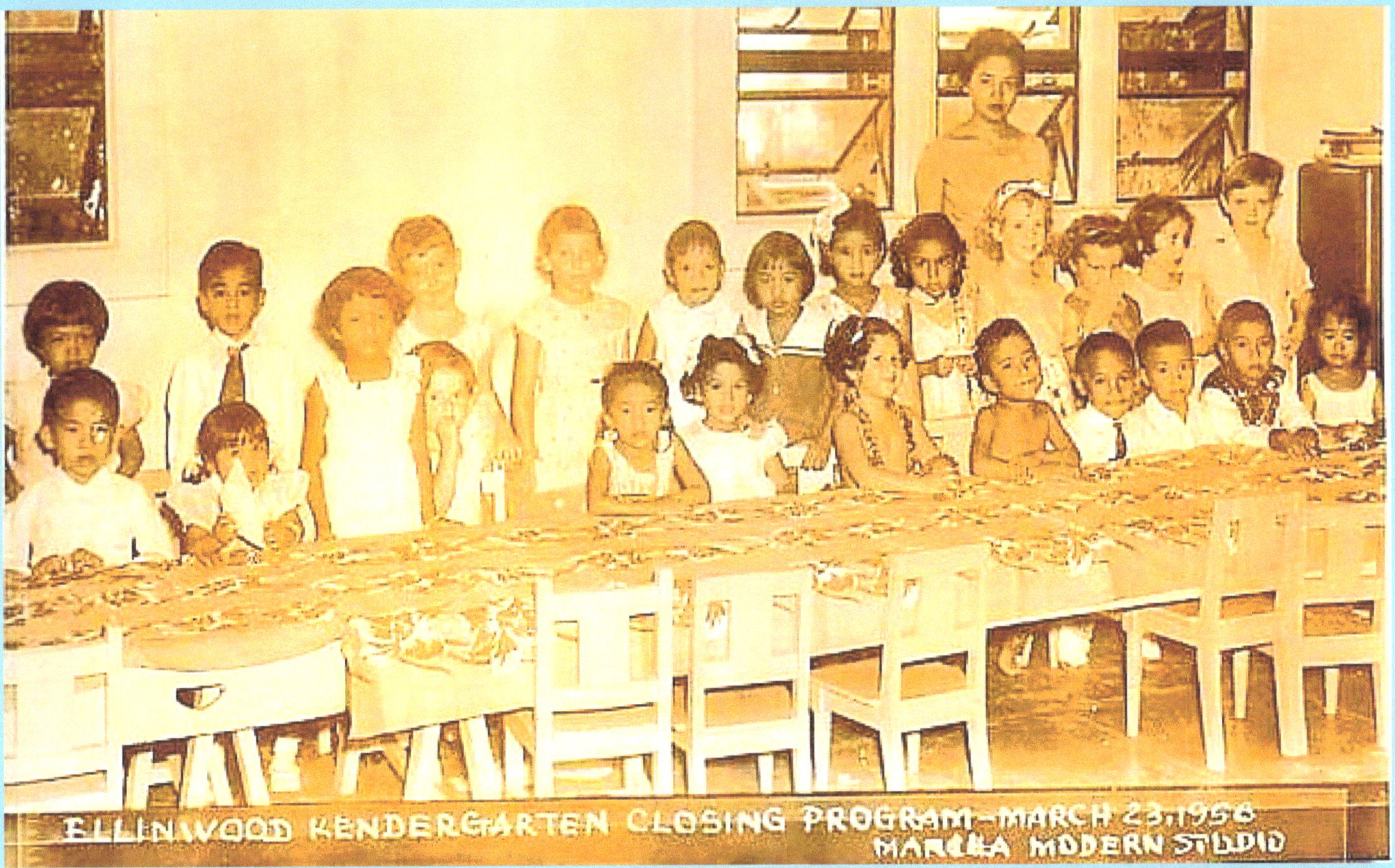

ELLINWOOD KENDERGARTEN CLOSING PROGRAM—MARCH 23, 1956
MANILA MODERN STUDIO

March 23, 1956 Pic - Ms. Cora Ramirez, 21, was teacher in Ellinwood Kindergarten School. Young Cynthia Guerrero, niece of Job Guerrero Elizes Jr. is shown in middle of seated row, in white dress and white hair ribbon.

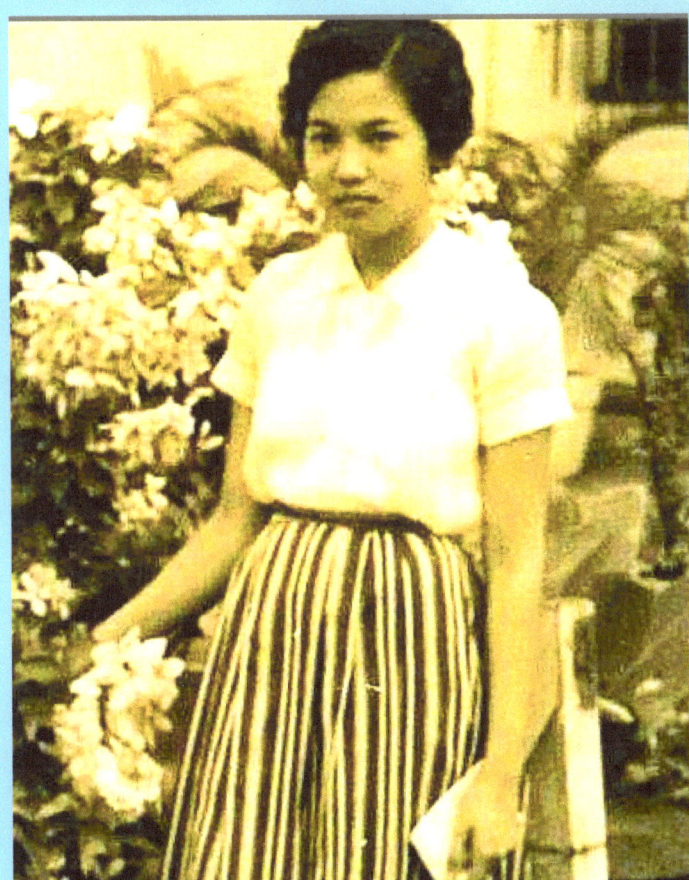

Circa 1954: Cora at 19

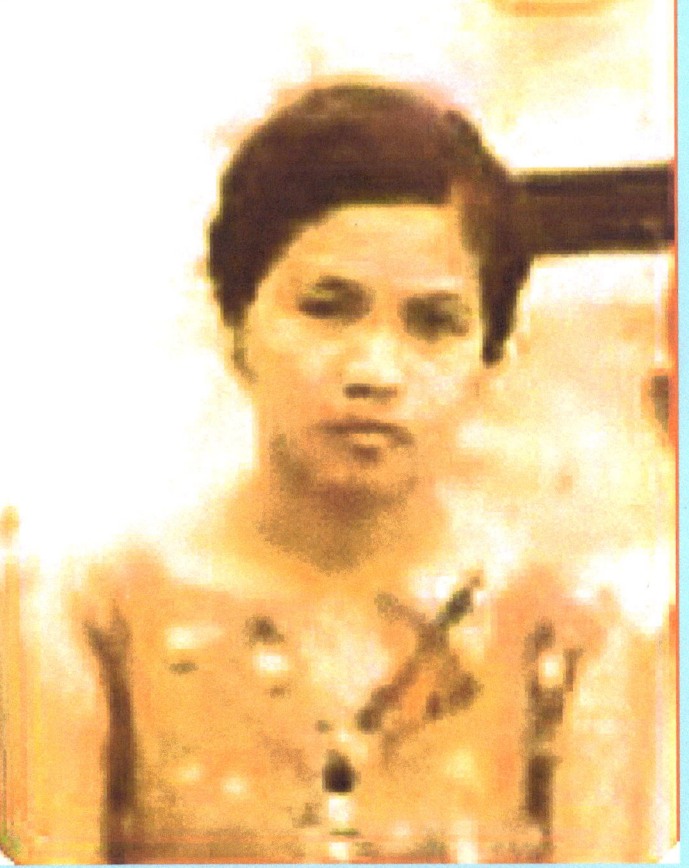

Circa 1952: Cora at 16

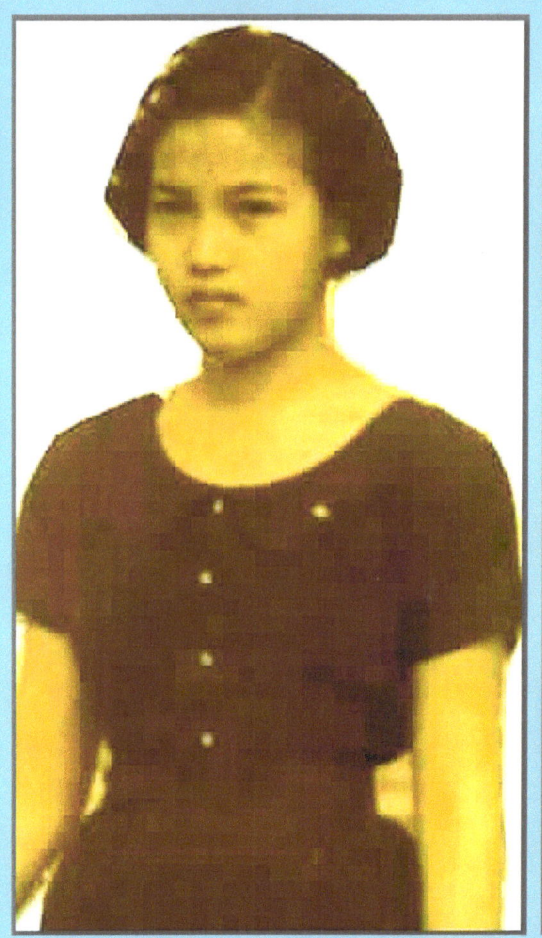
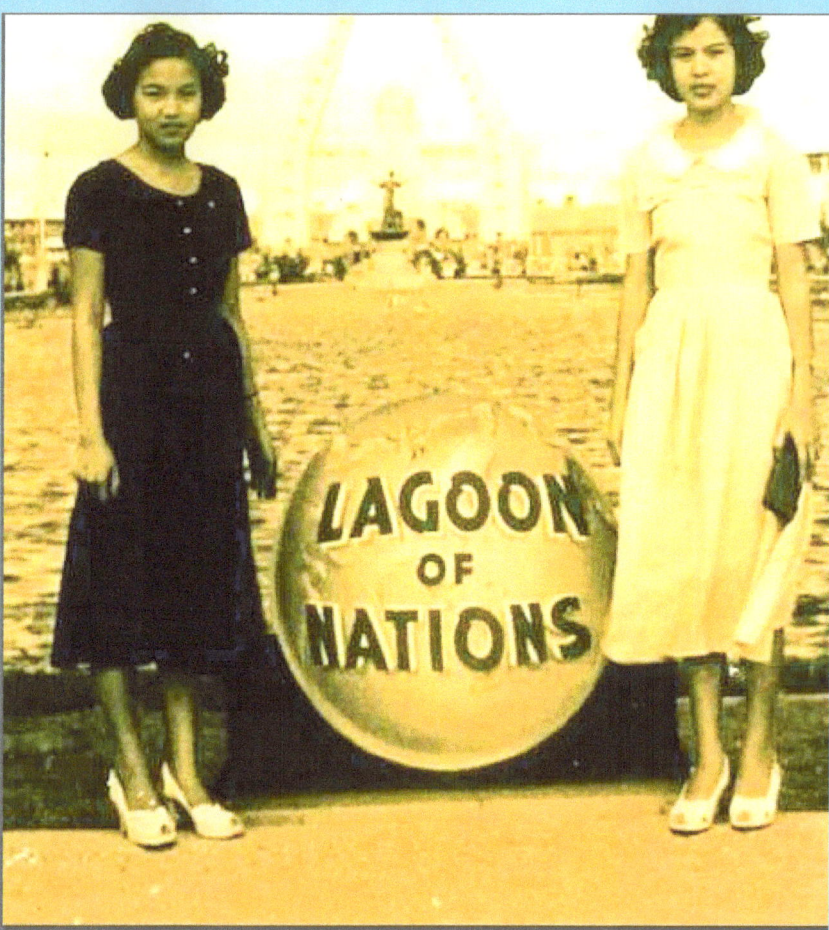

1952: Cora at 17 + + + Cora & Priscilla Javier at Rizal or Luneta Park during Phil. Intl. Fair

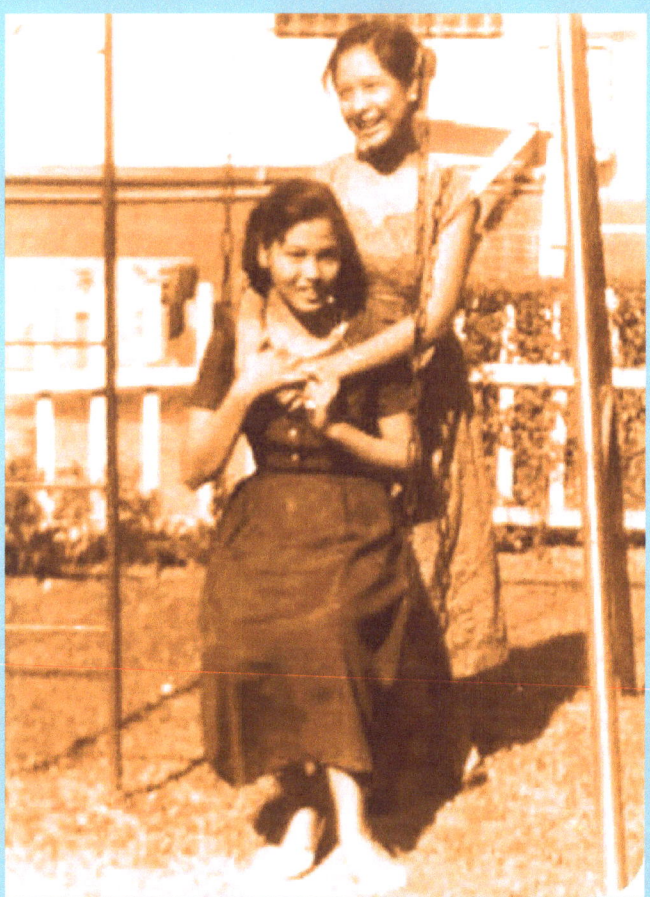
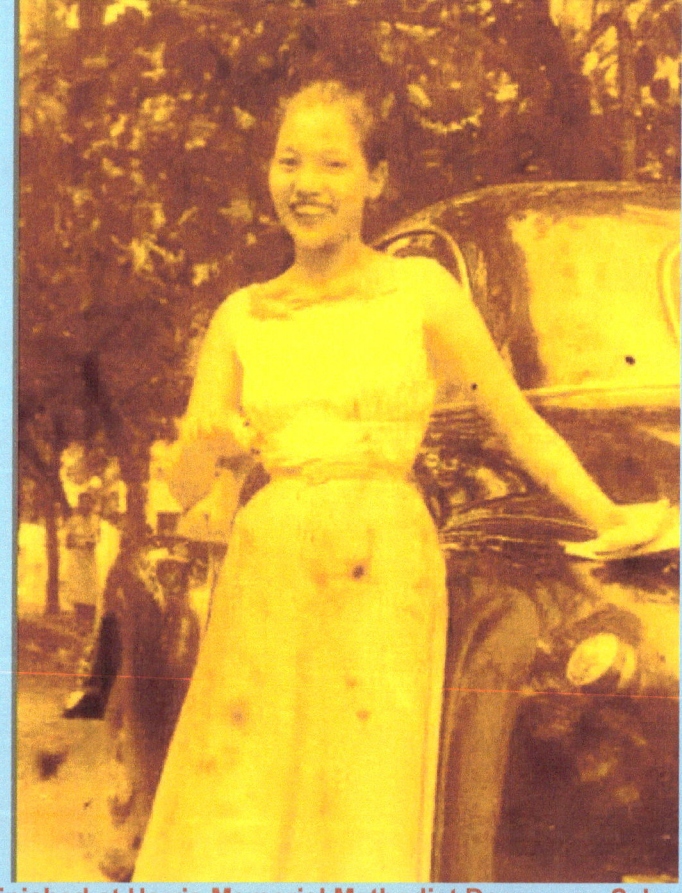

1952-53: Cora at 18 with Naty Bote Reyes + solo. Cora finished at Harris Memorial Methodist Deaconess School

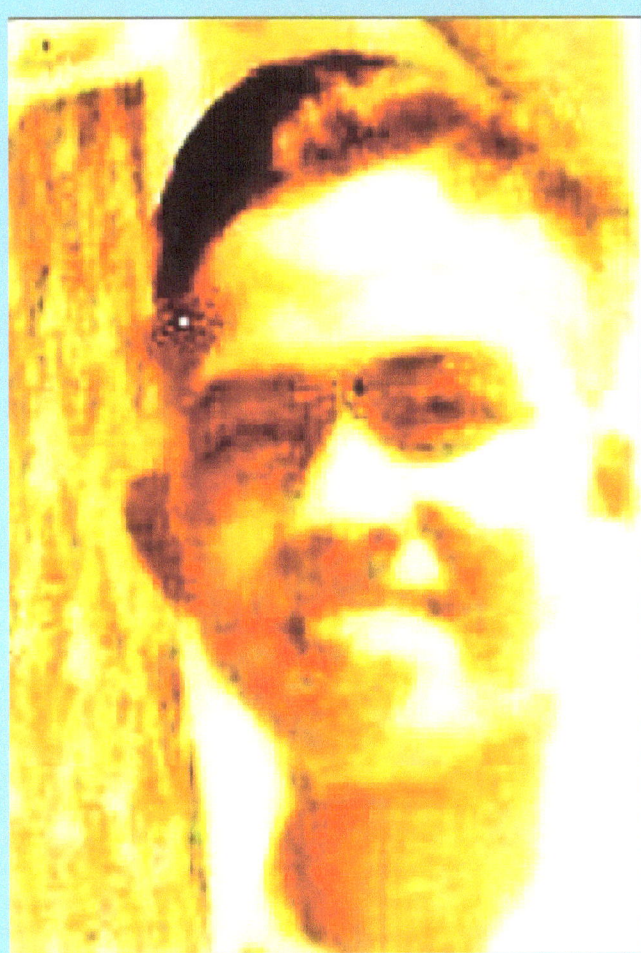
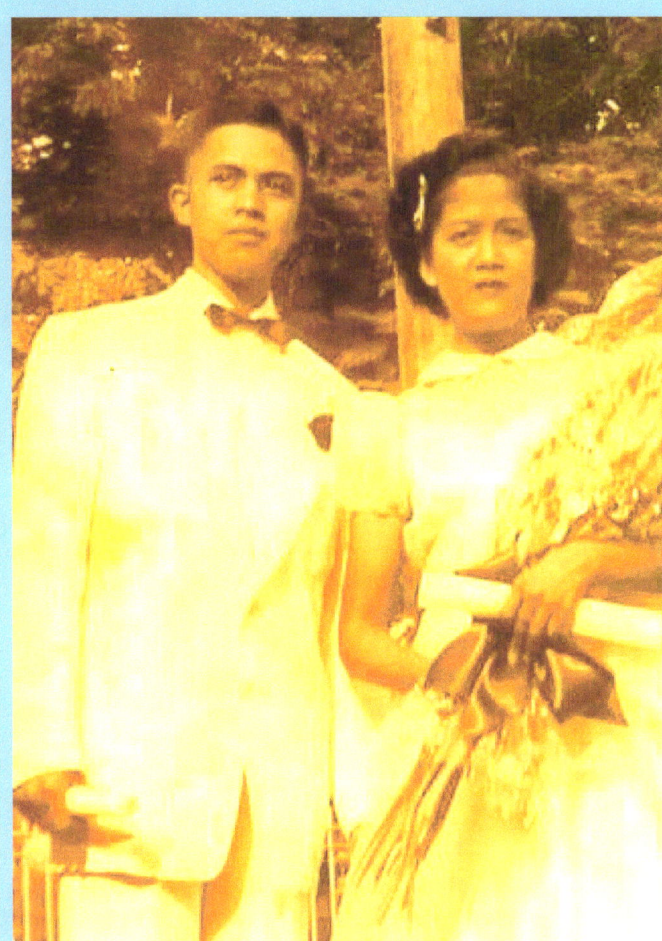

Job at 18, 1st Yr at Mapua Engineering + + 1951: Job at 17 & Sister Susan, 18 at HS Graduation in Pasay

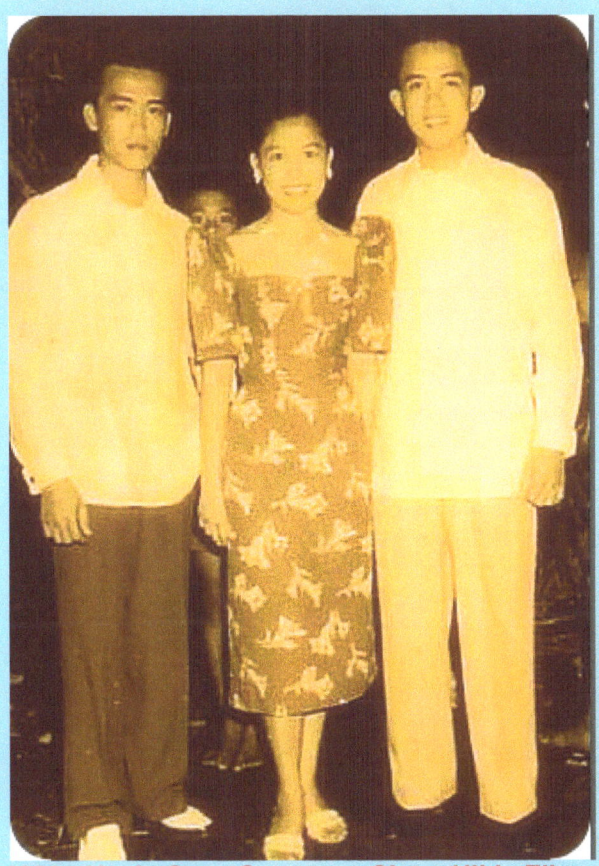
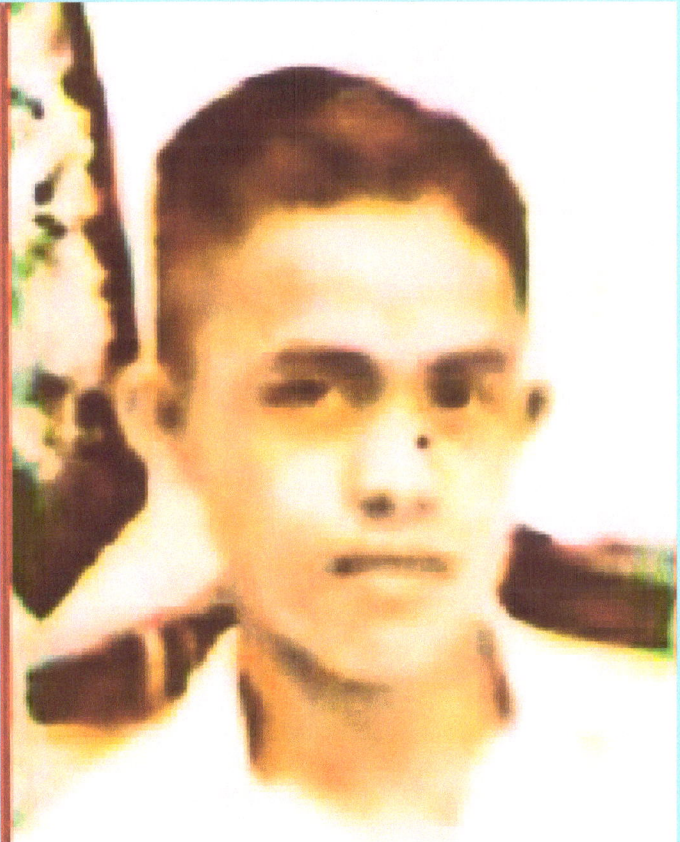

1956: Uncle Gene Guerrero+ Sister Hilda Elizes + Job at 22 + + + 1953: Job at 19,in Mapua Engineering

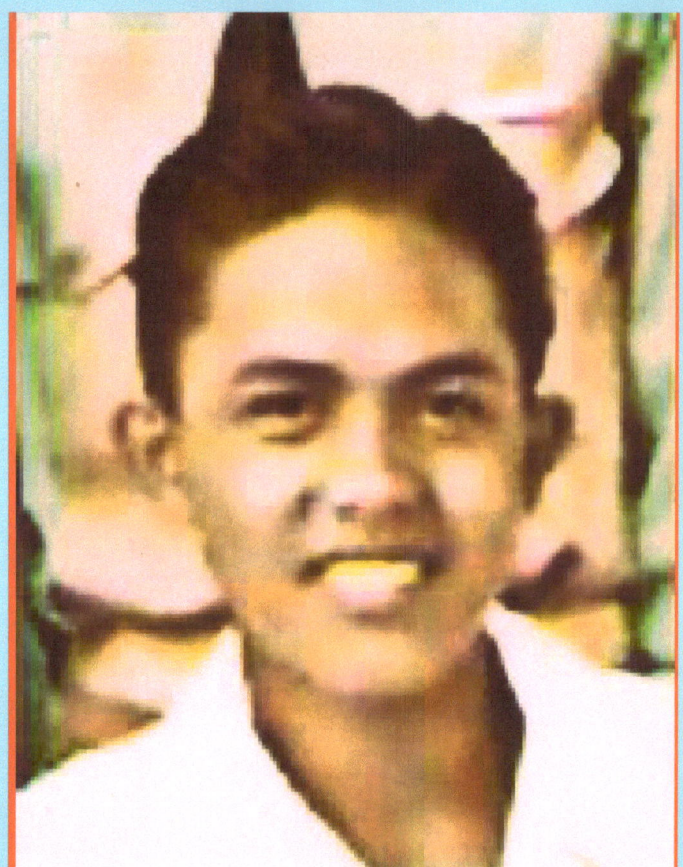
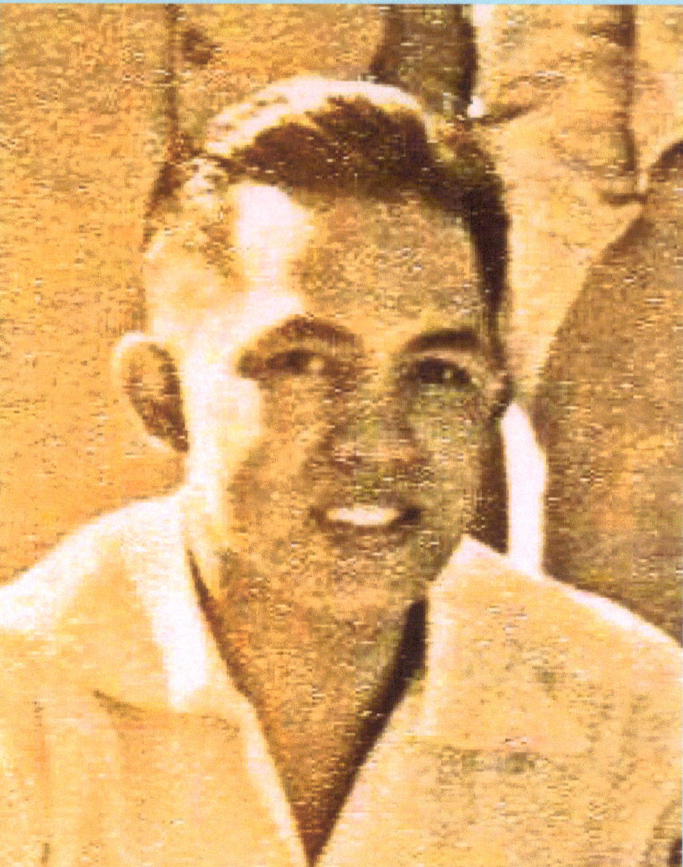
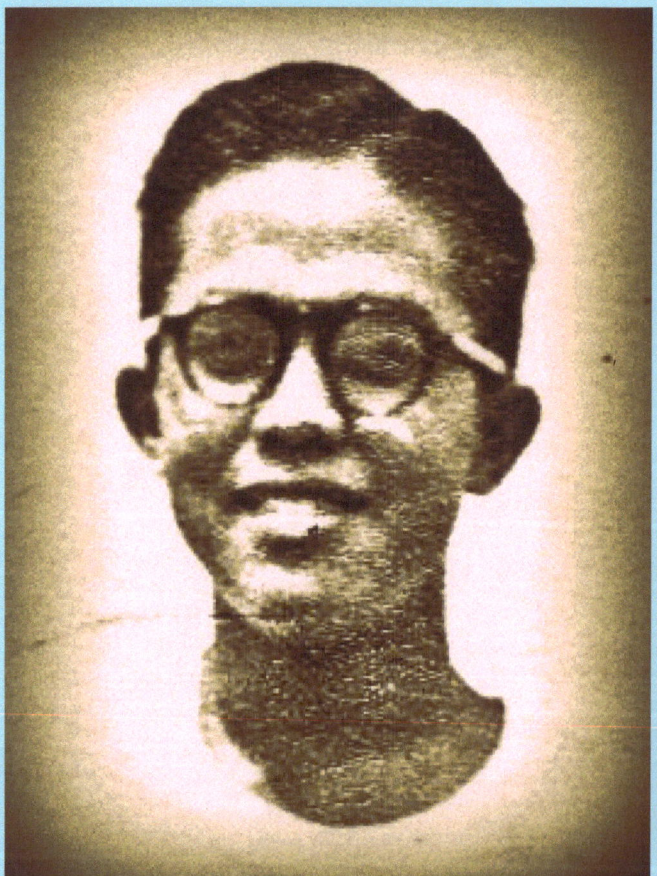
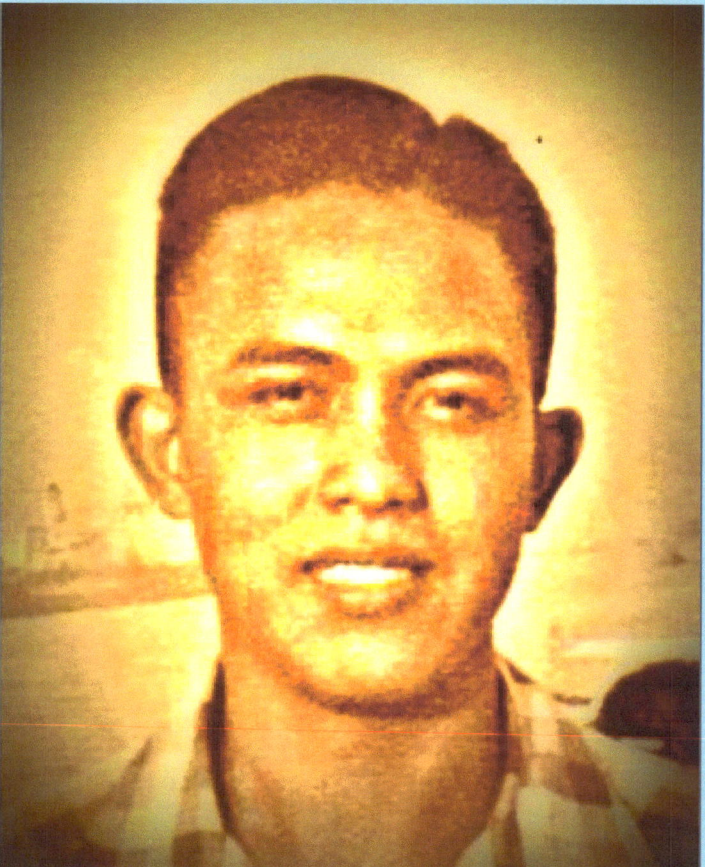

1952-1956: Young Job at 17-22, while working at Philippine Christian College as Clerk and studying at Mapua Engineering as night student.

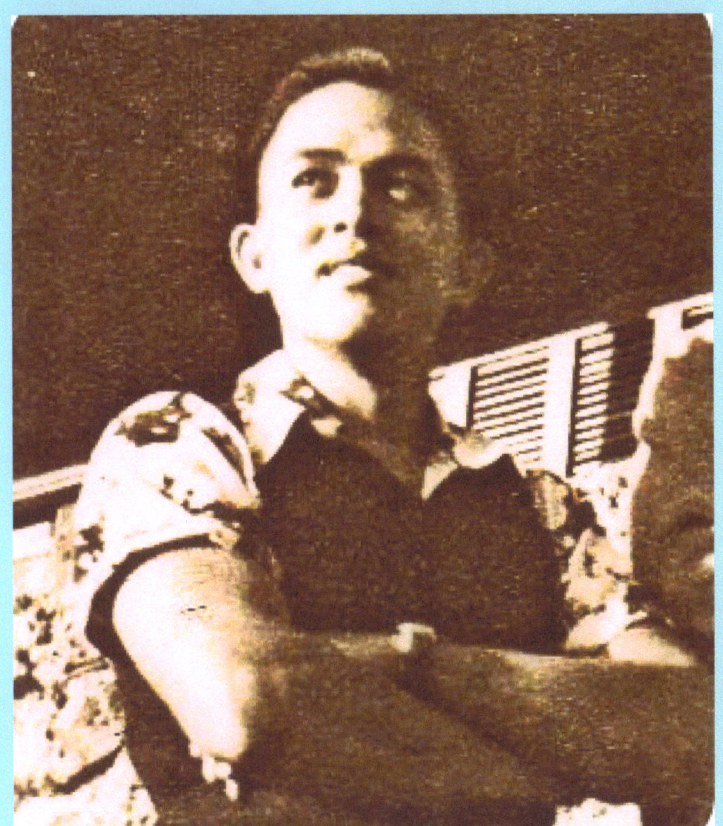
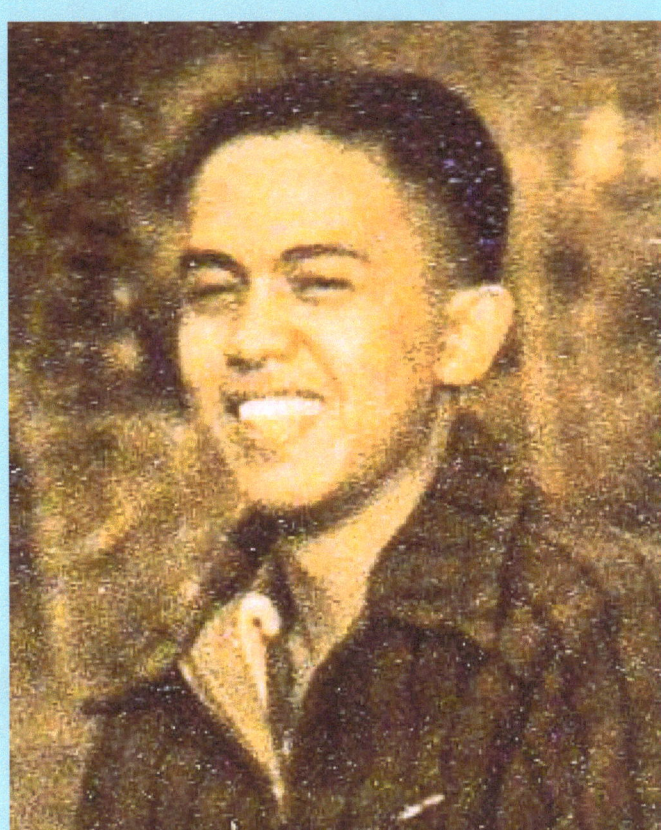

1952-54: Young Job at 17-18

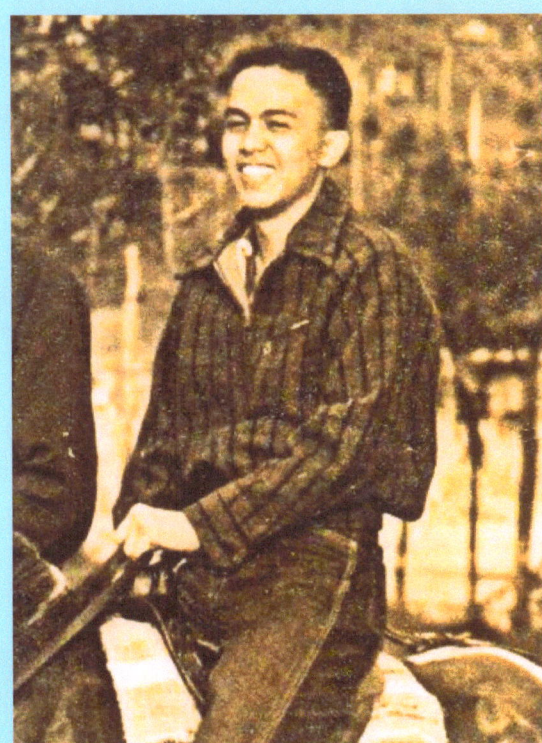

1953: Job at 19 in Baguio

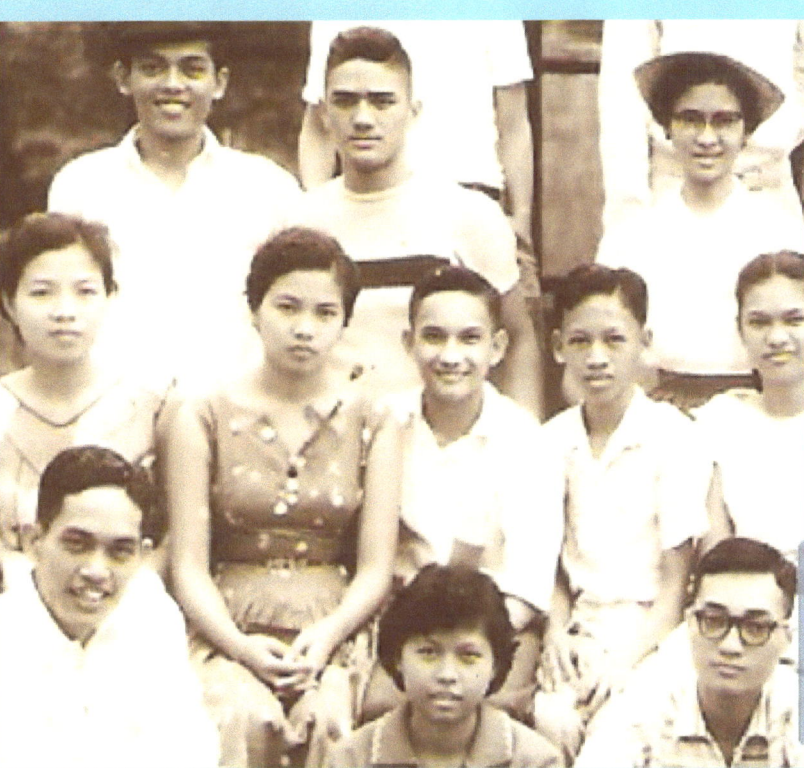

1953: Cora at 18 with Ellinwood Christian Youth Group

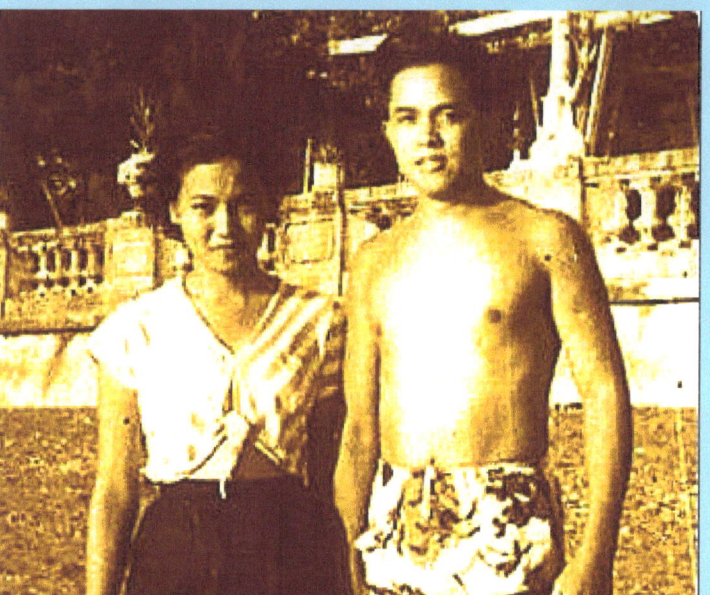

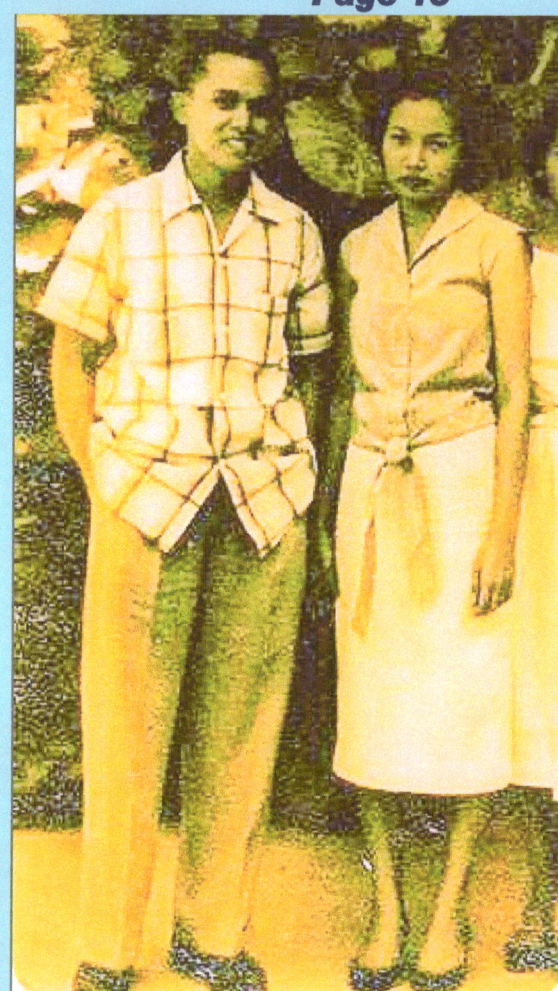

1958: Job and Cora, engaged to be married

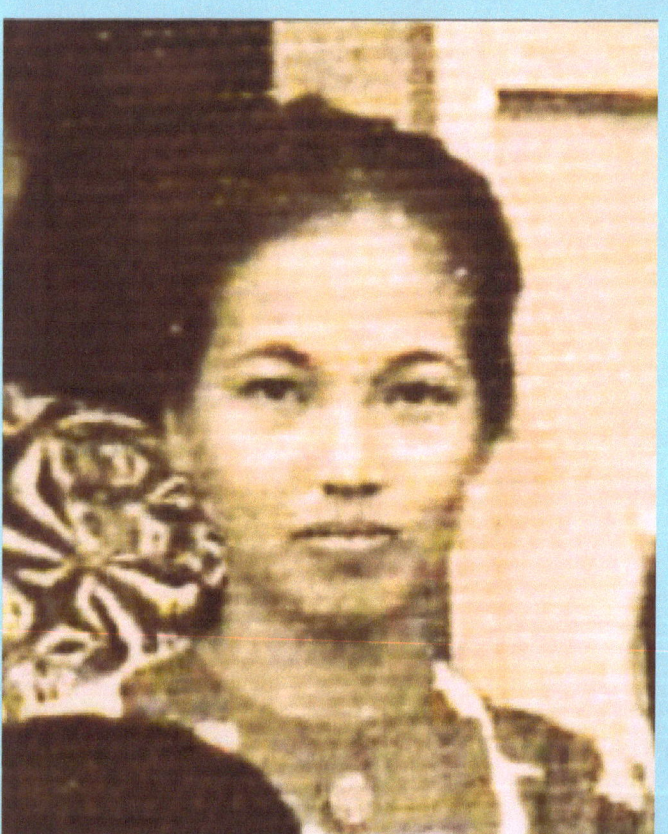

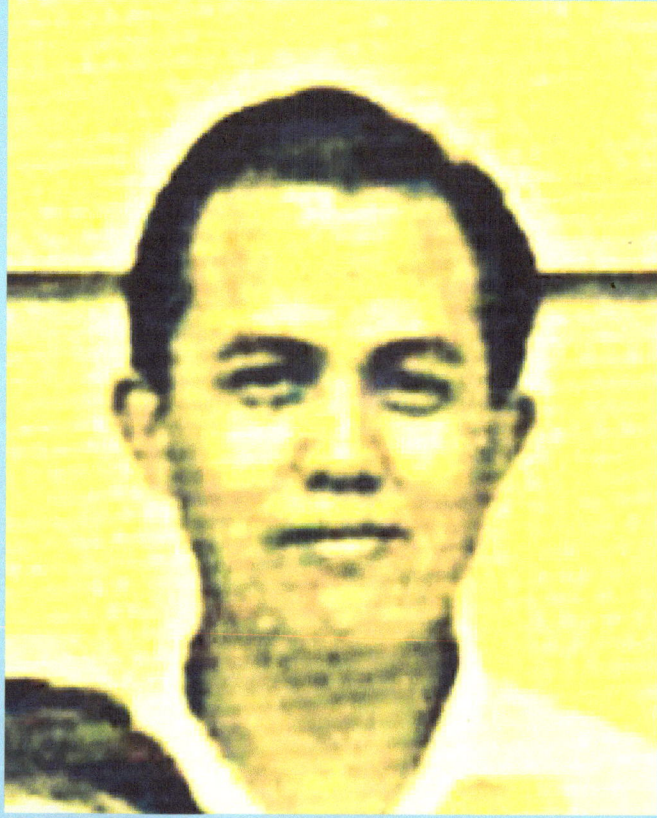

1961: Cora & Job, married (had first baby)

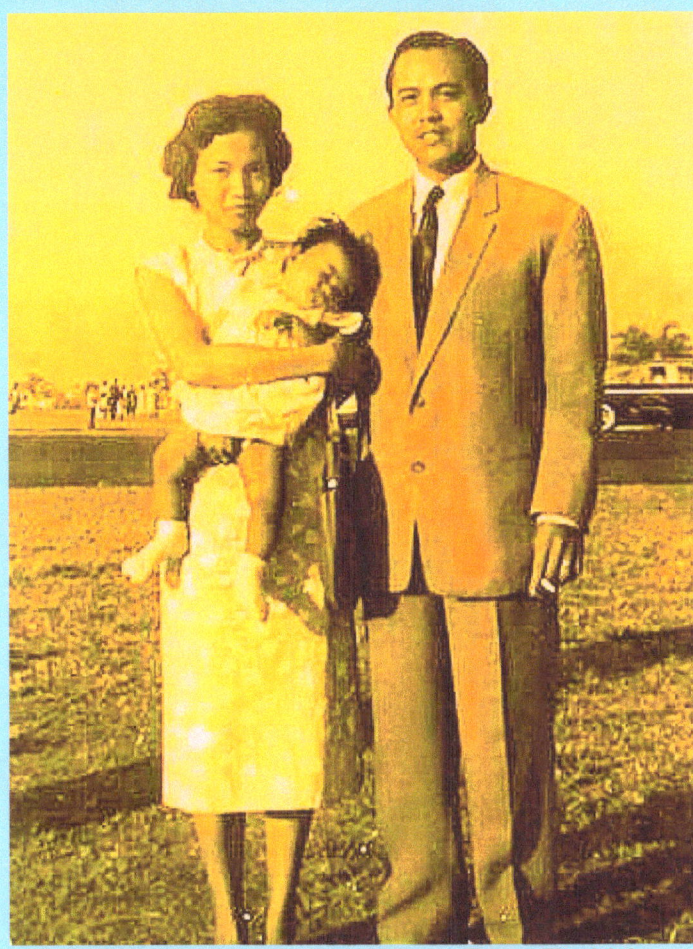

1961: Job and Cora and Baby Ester (Techie)

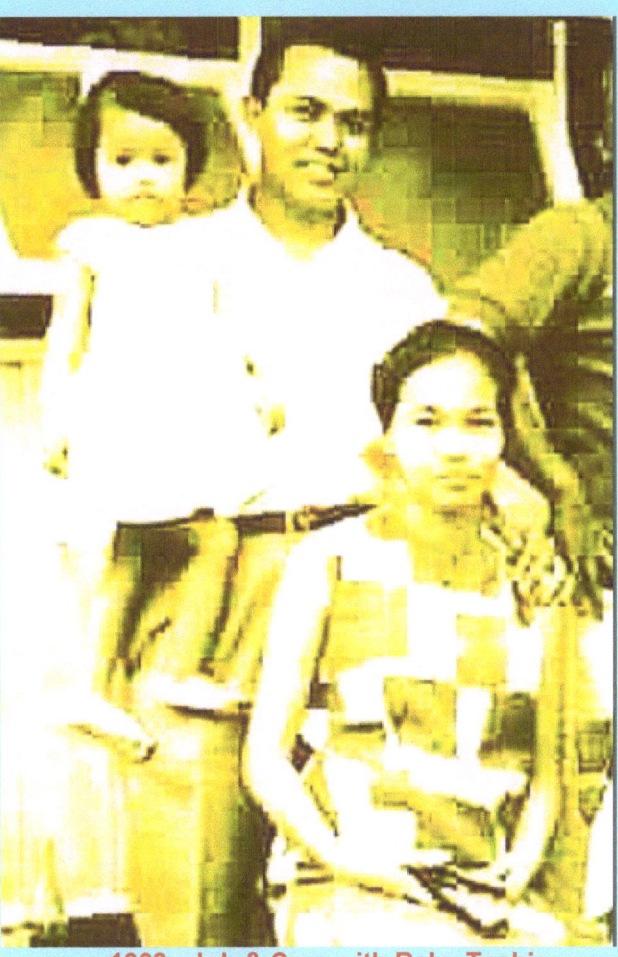

1962: Job & Cora with Baby Techie

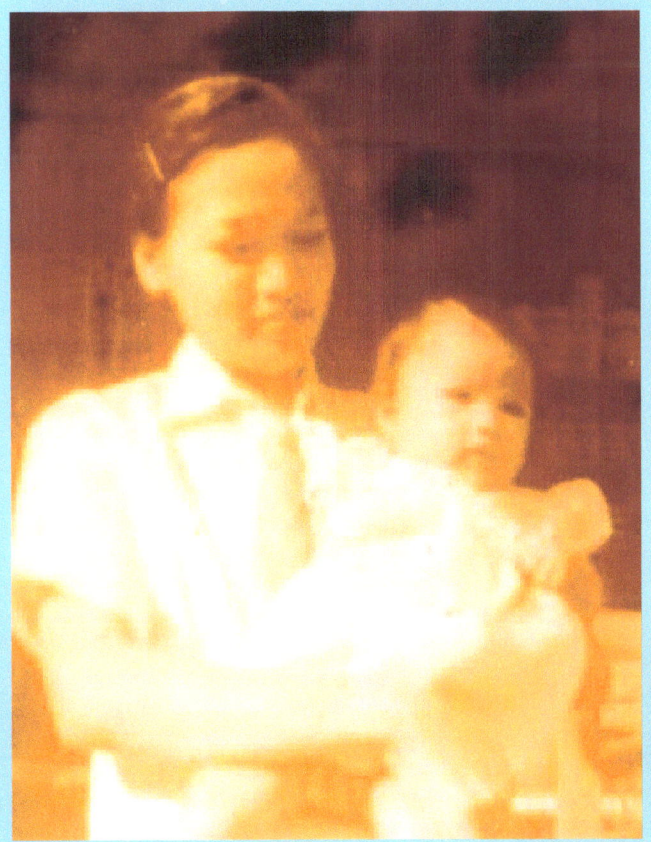

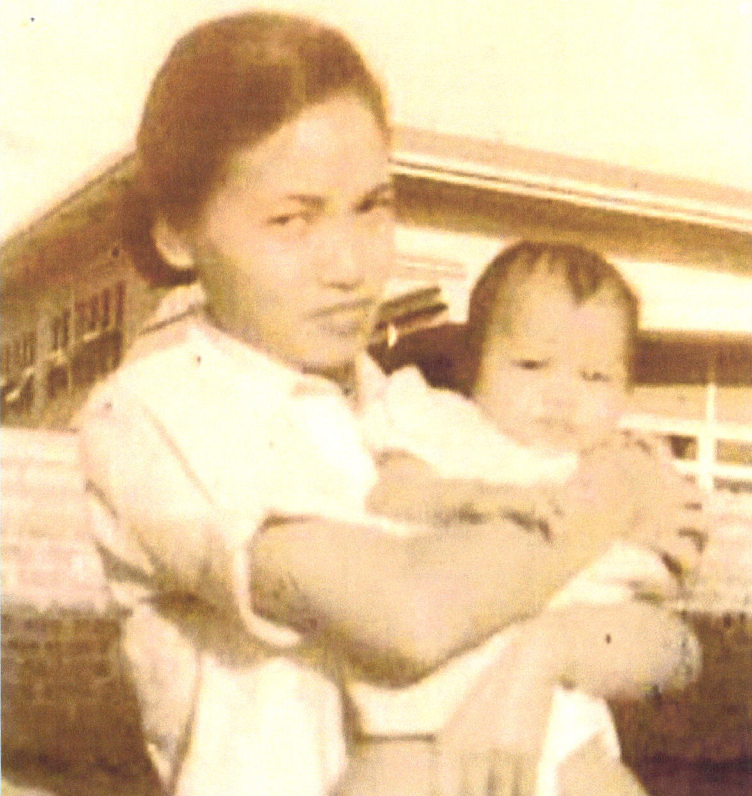

1961: Cora and first child Techie

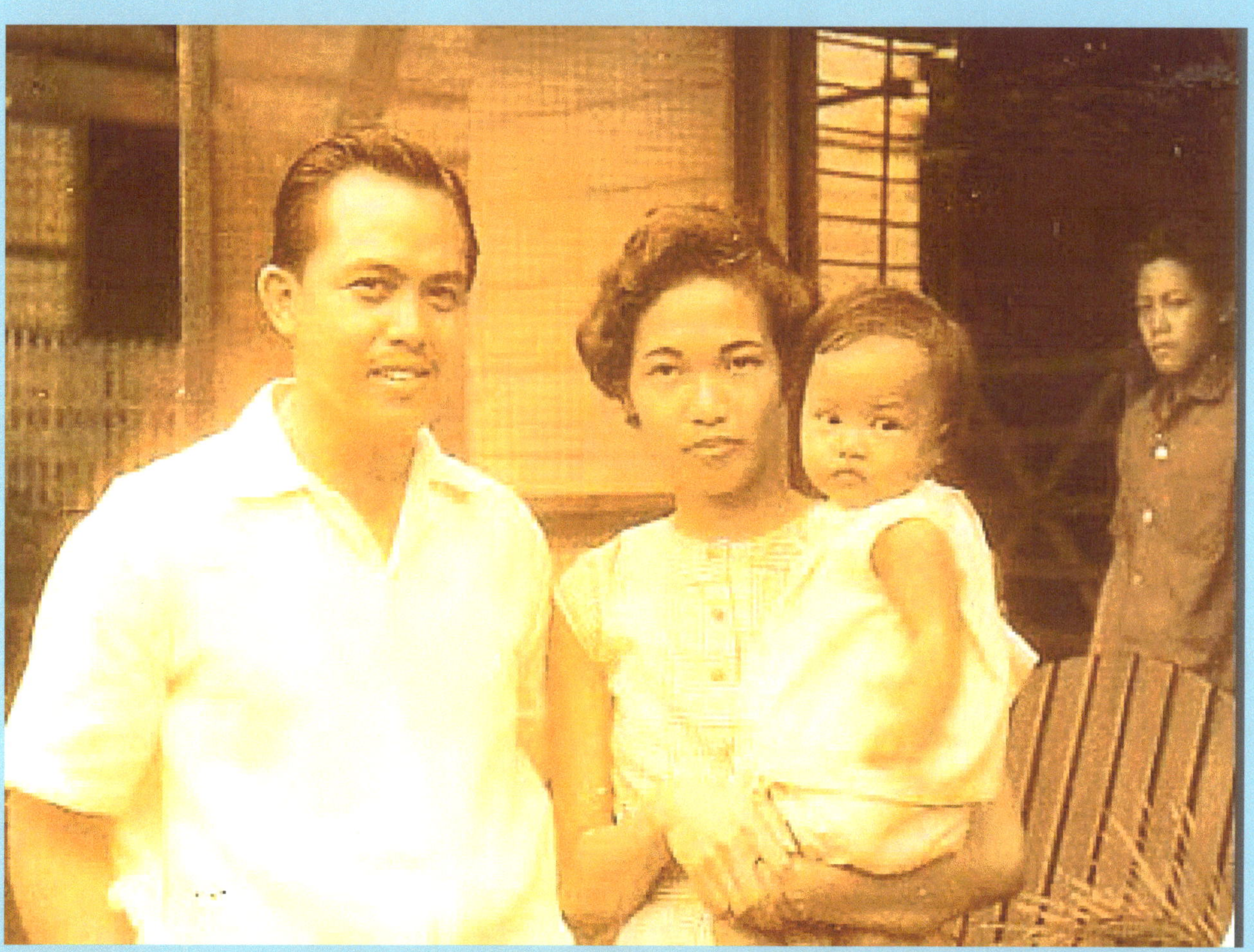

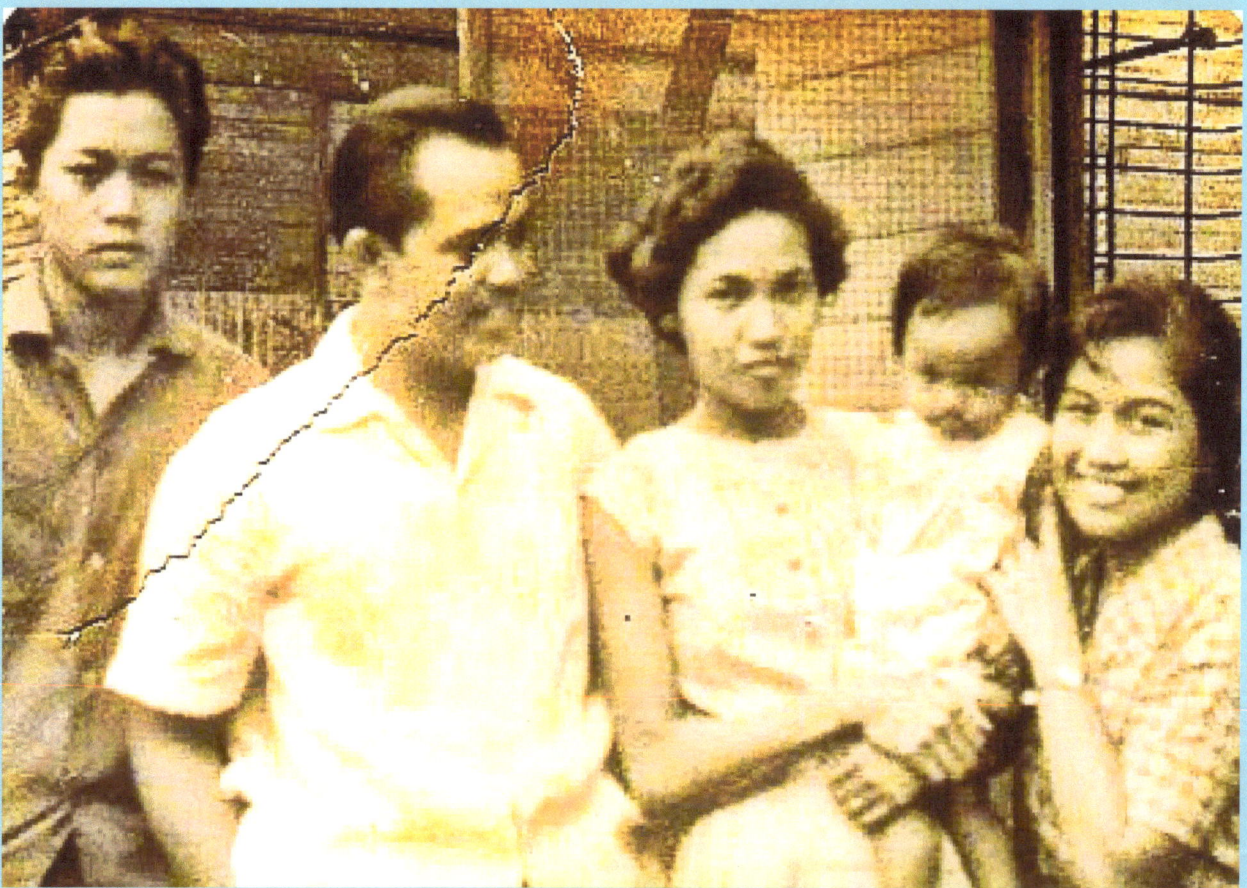

1962 Pics: Job & Cora with Baby Techie + Job's brother Bobby and sister Hilda

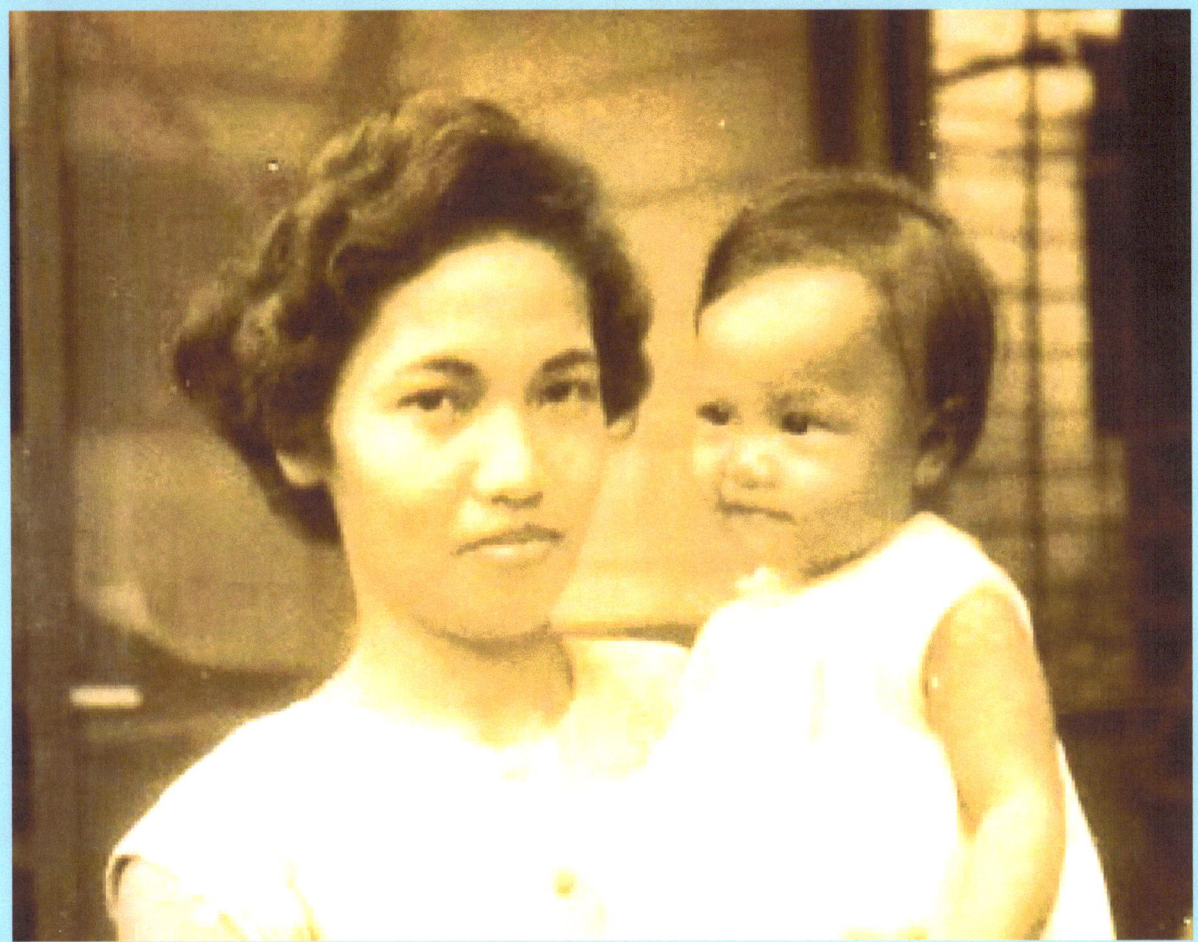

Nanay Cora and Baby Techie, age 1

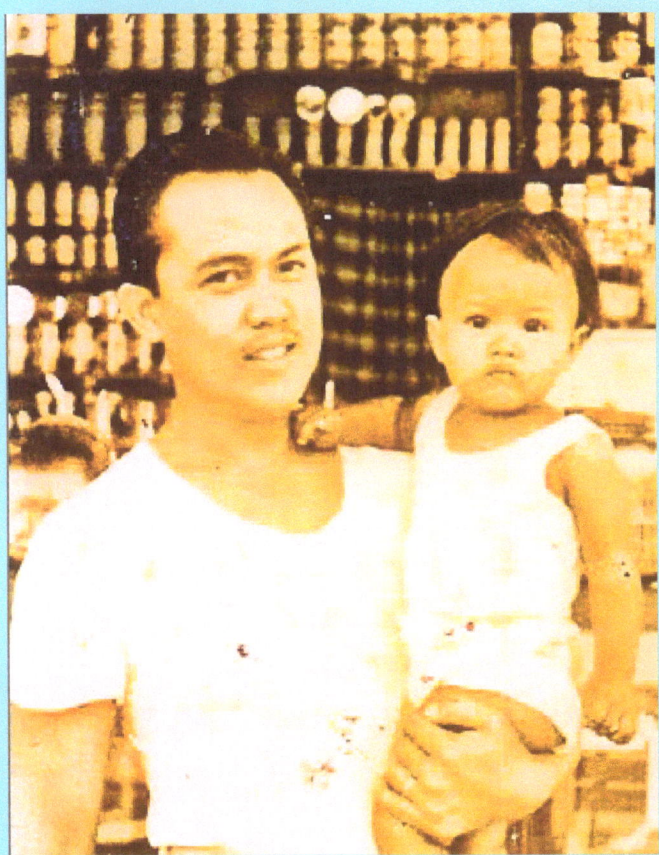

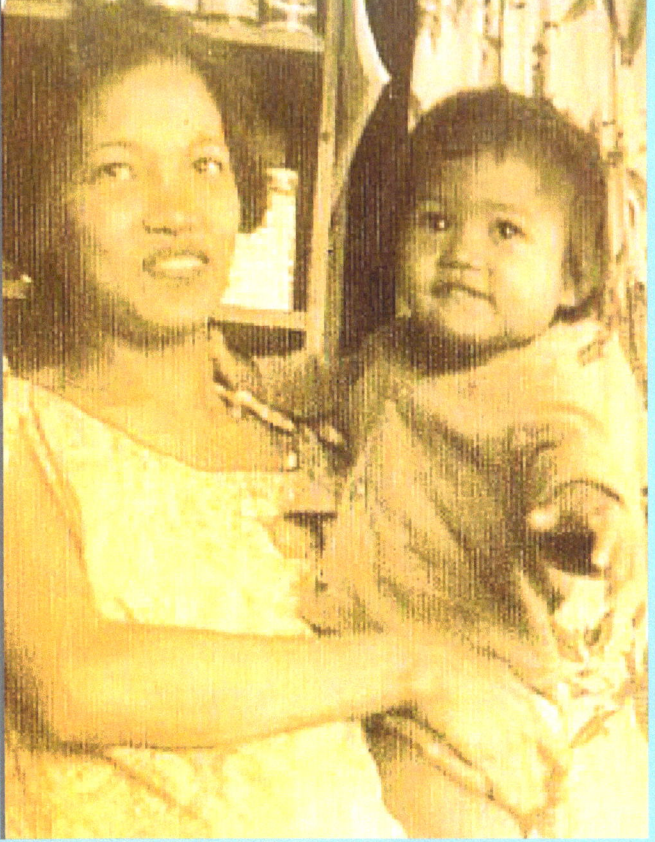

Baby Techie (Ester) at Age 1, with young Tatay Job and Nanay Cora

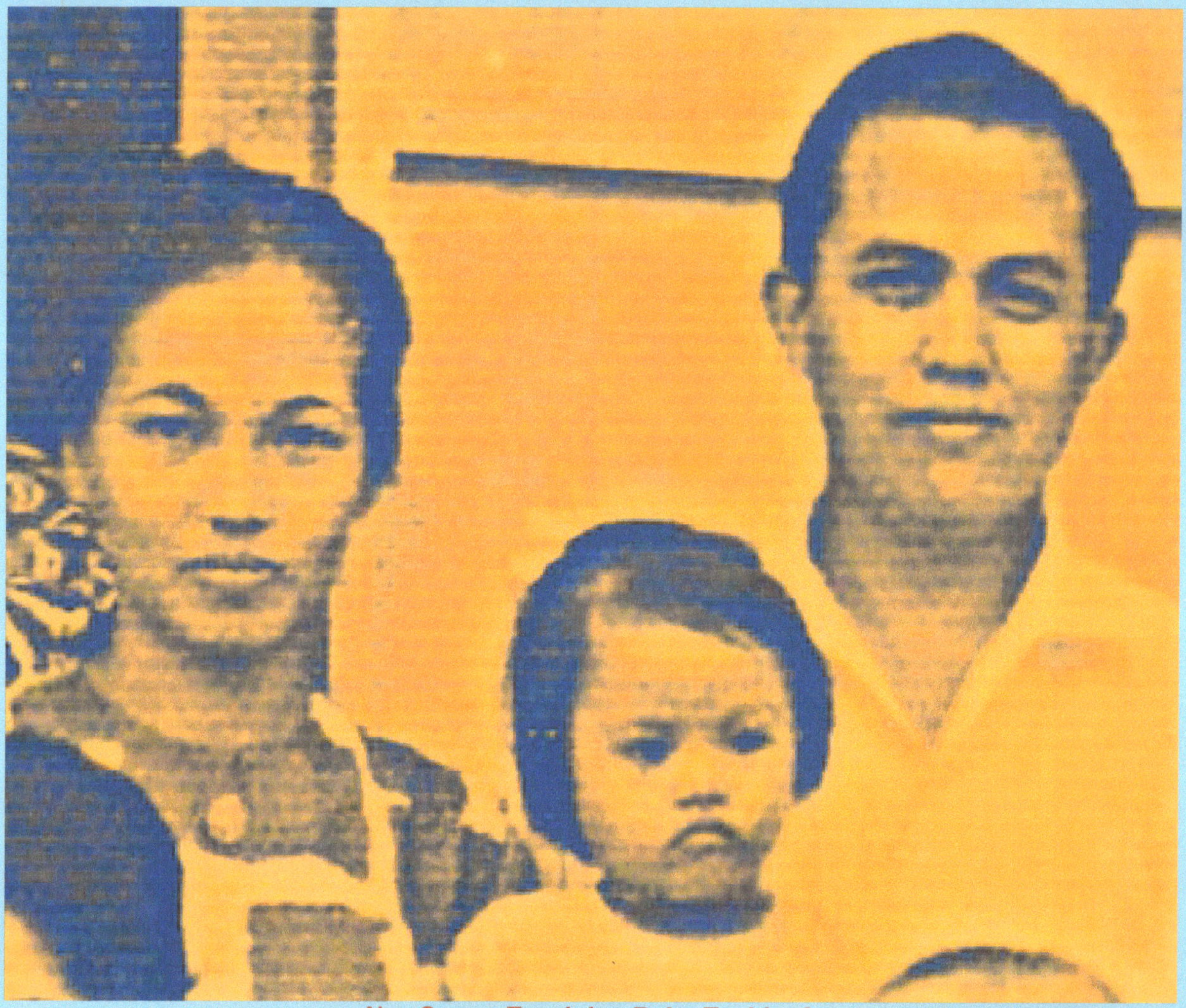

Nay Cora + Tay Job + Baby Techie, 2

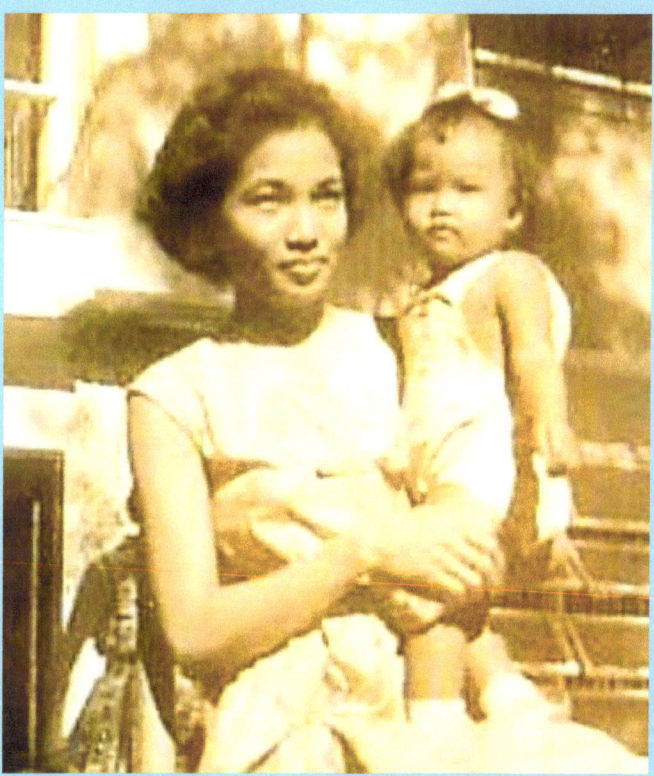

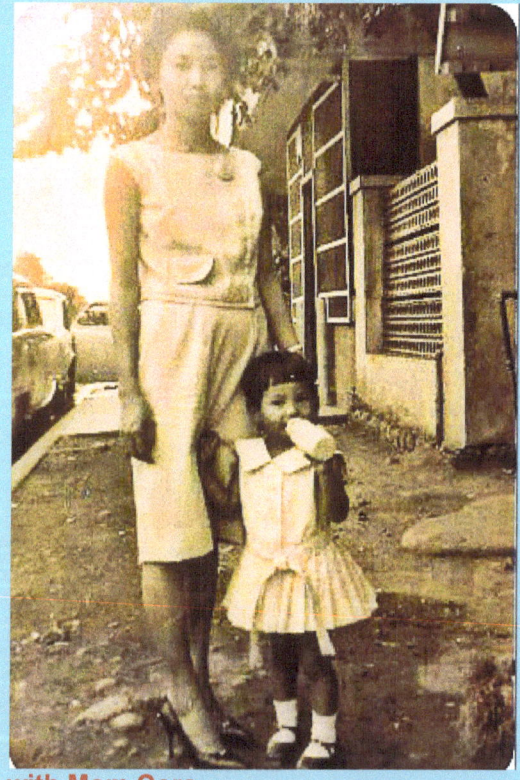

1962 Pics: Young Techie at Age 2 with Mom Cora

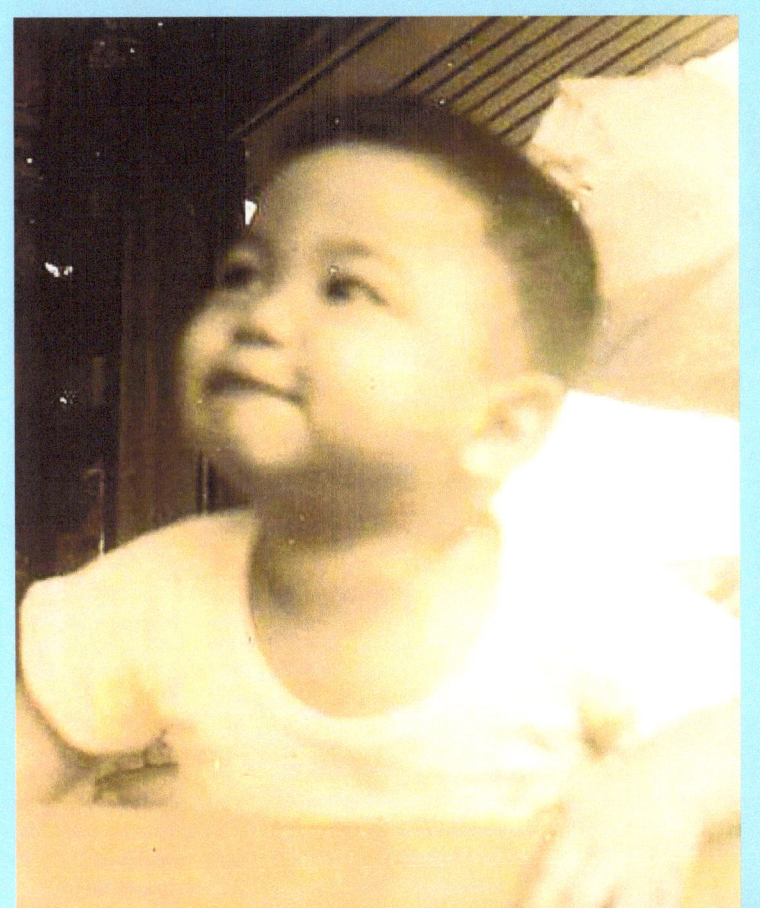
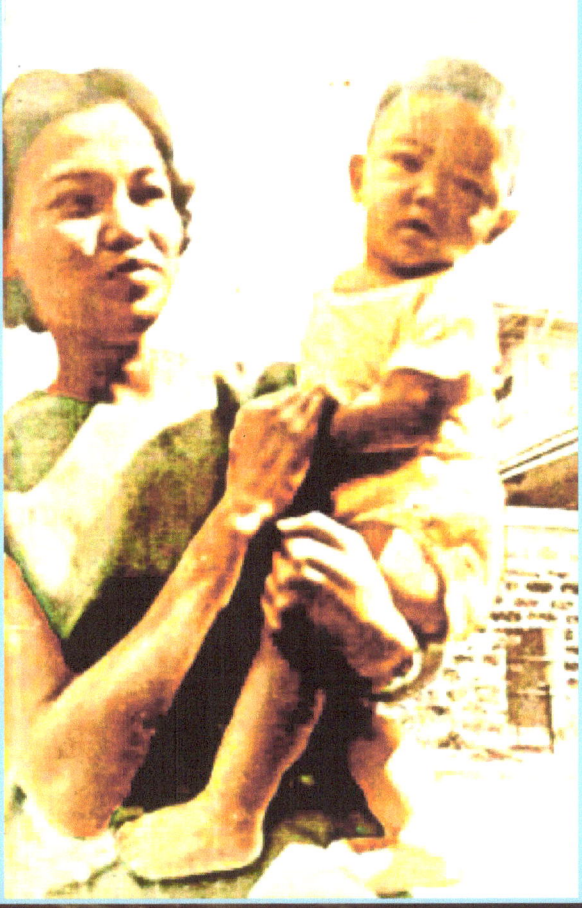
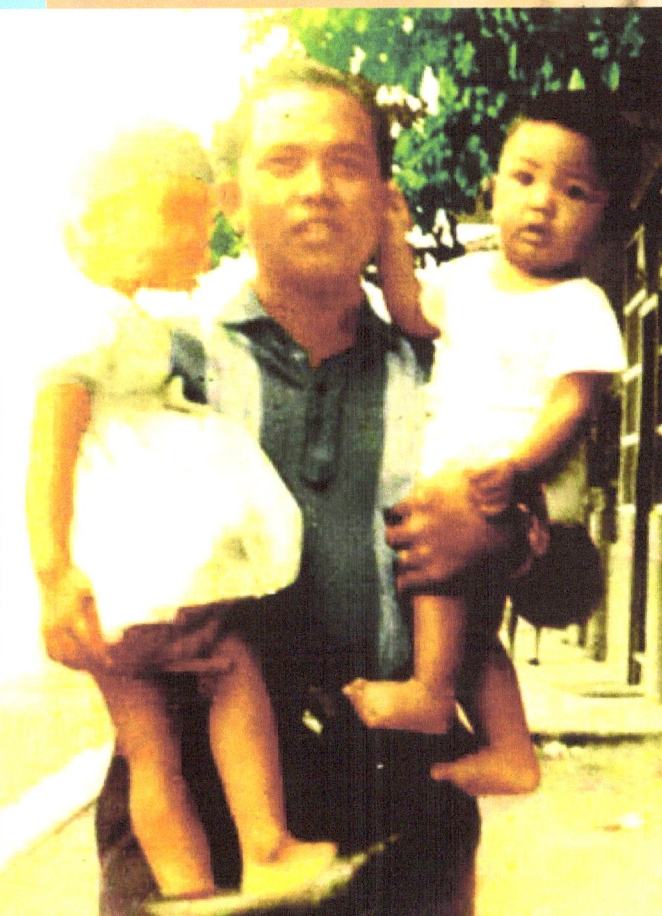
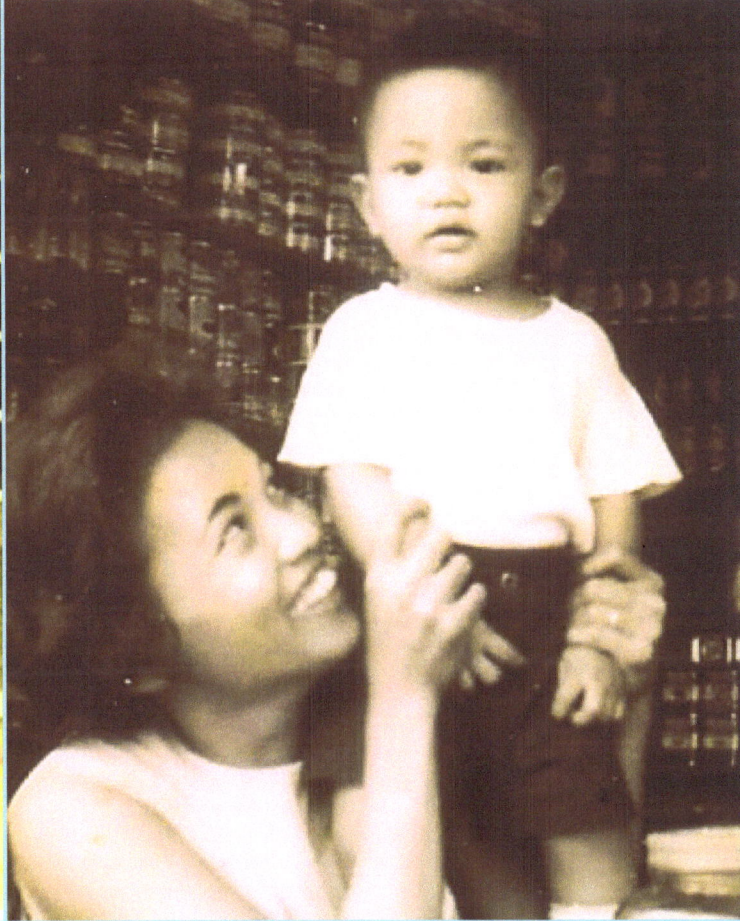

1963 Pics: Baby Chevy (Chevalier) at Age 1 and Techie at age 2 with Tatay Job and Nanay Cora

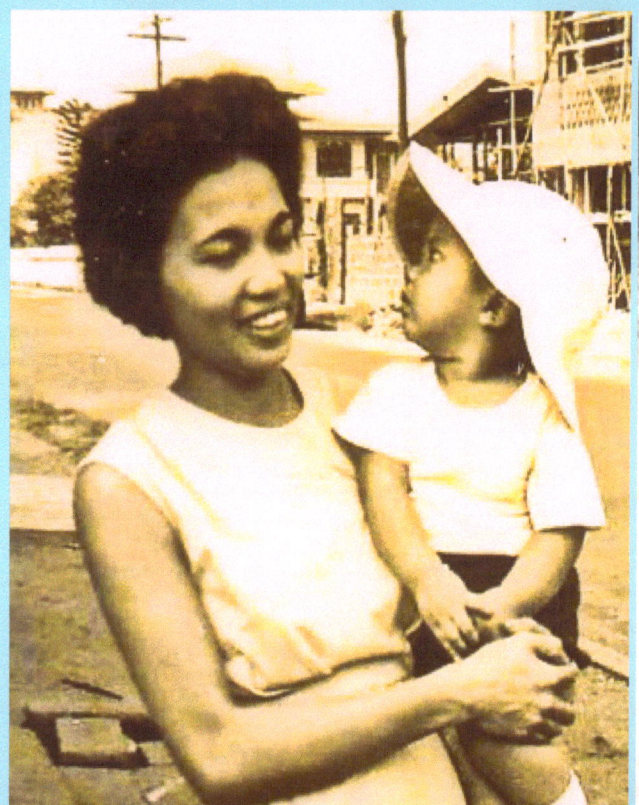
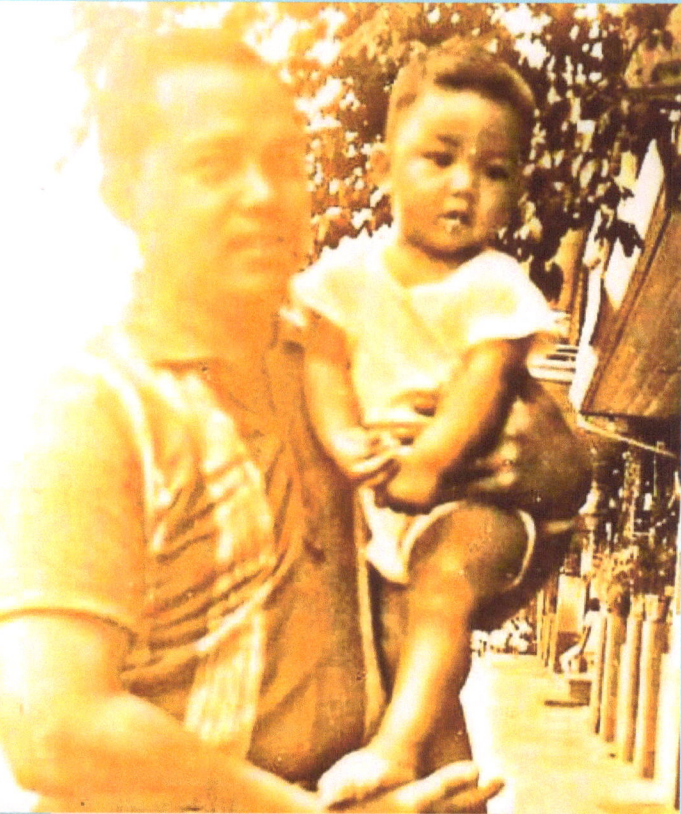
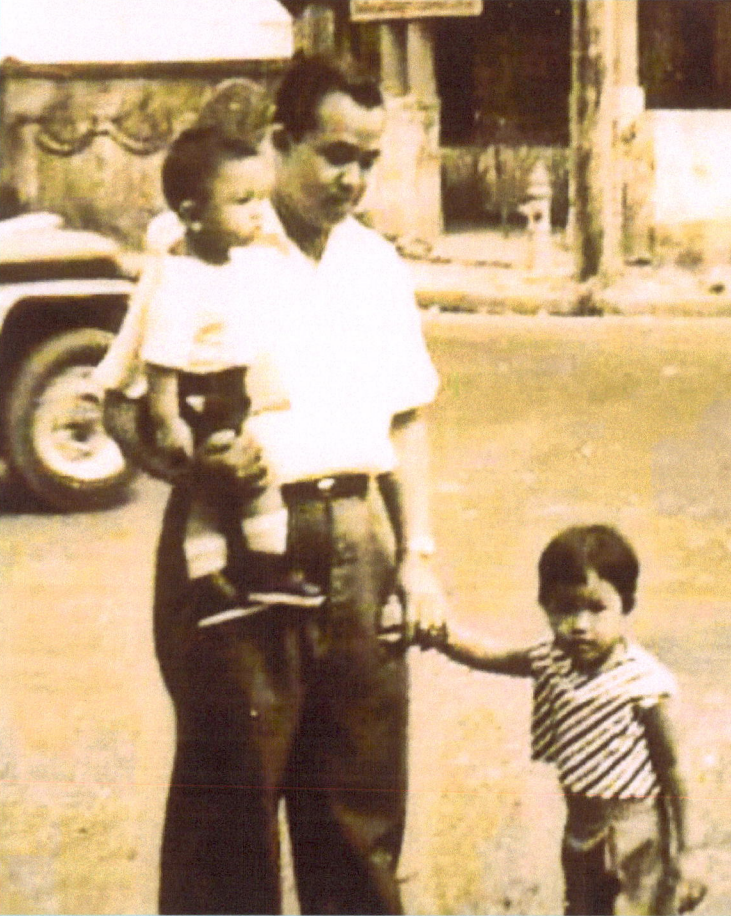
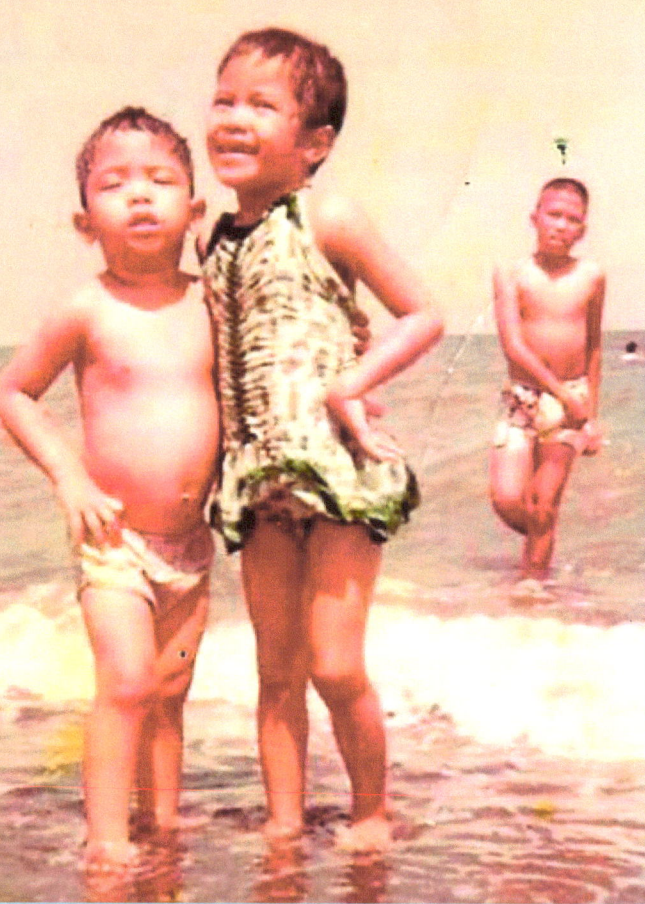

Several Pictures showing Young Chevy and Young Techie with Tatay Job & Nanay Cora
+ their nephew Noel Ferrer

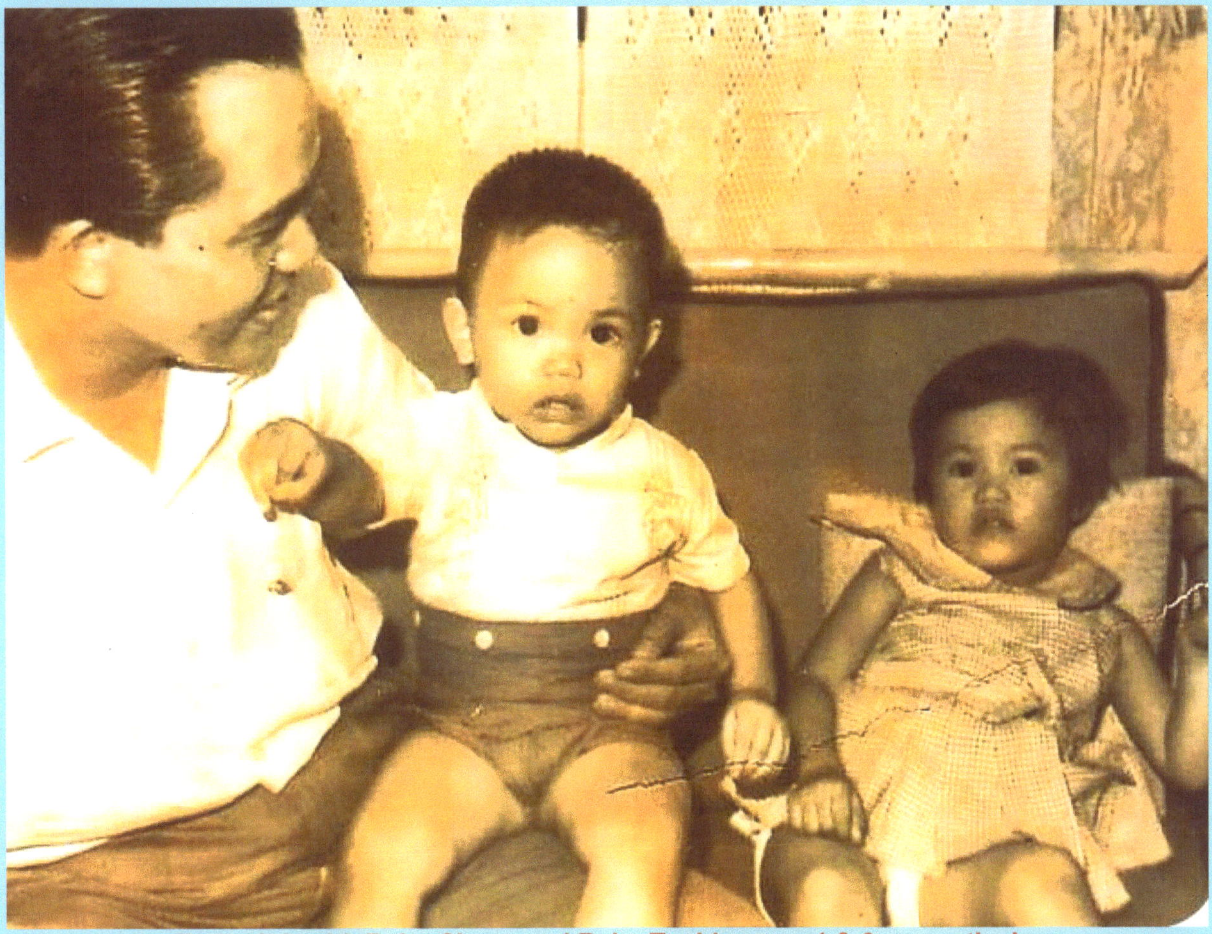

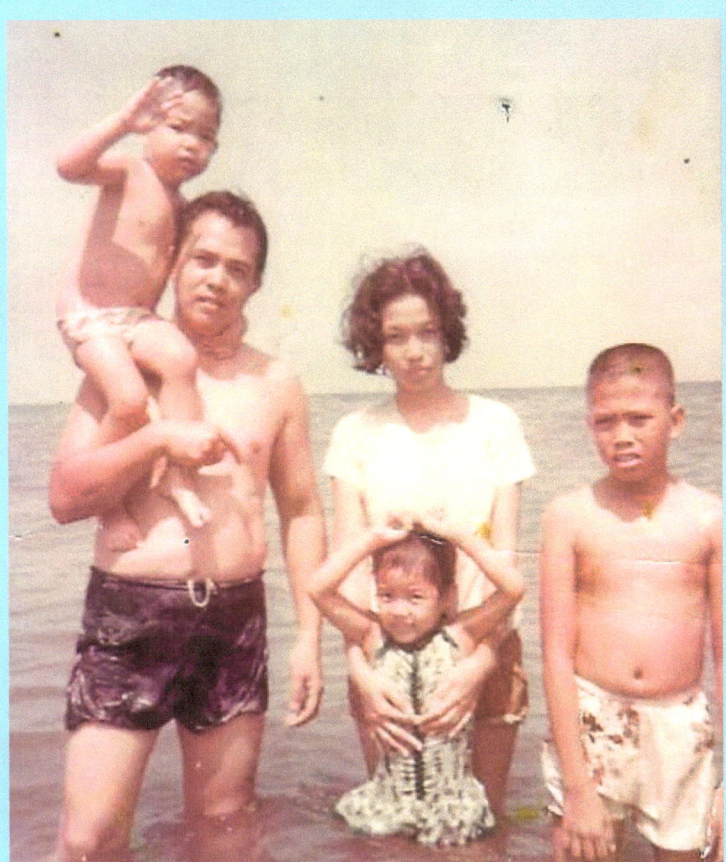

Tatay Job with Baby Chevy and Baby Techie, ages 1 & 3 respectively.

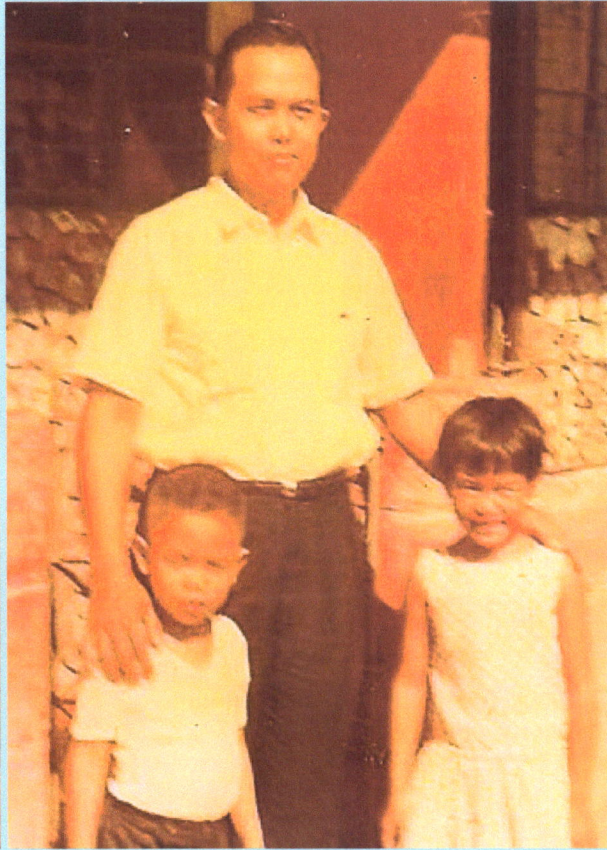

Tay Job & Nay Cora with Baby Chevy,1 + Techie,3 + Noel Ferrer,9 . . . + Tay Job with Chevy, 2 + Techie,4

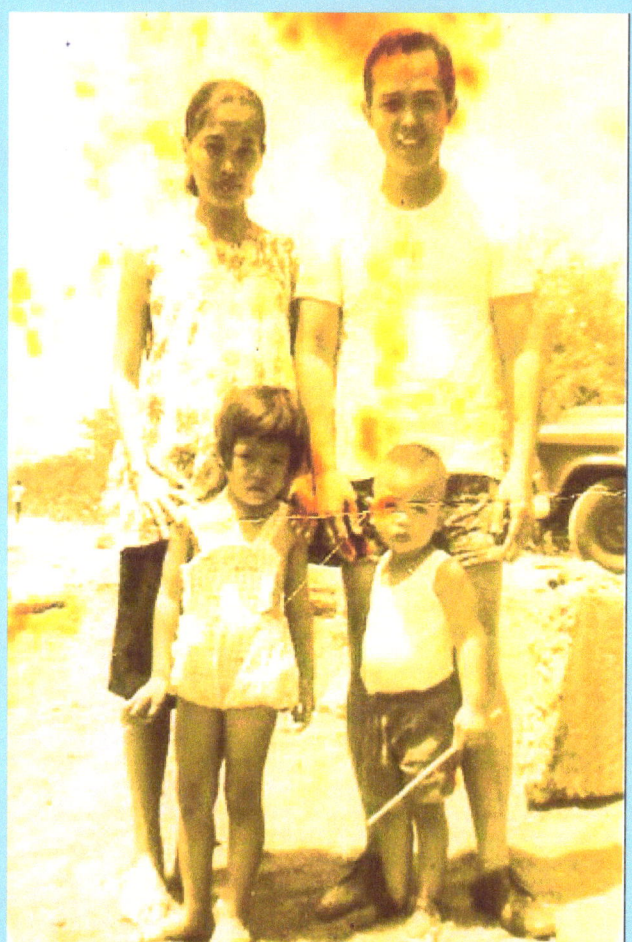

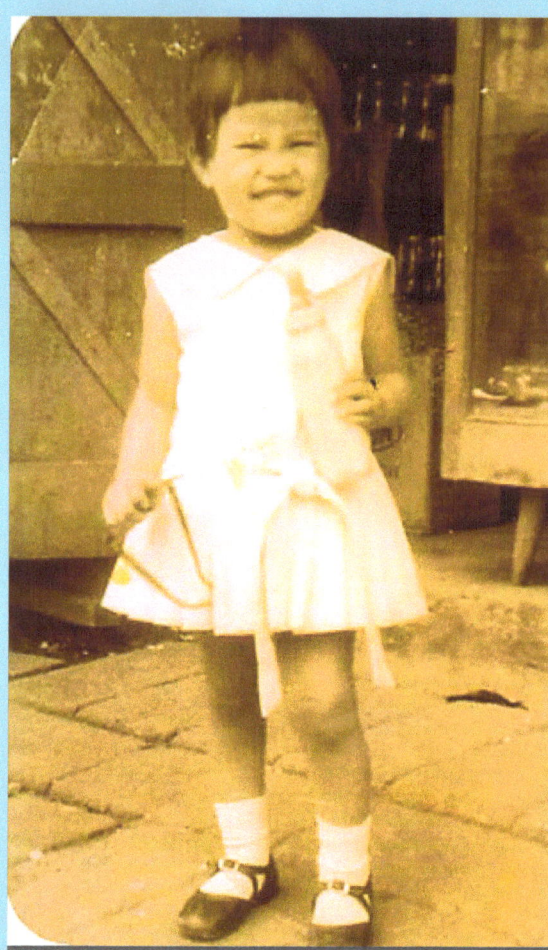

Nay Cora, preggy with Sharon (still birth) + Tay Job with Young Techie, 3 & Baby Chevy,1 . . . + Techie,4

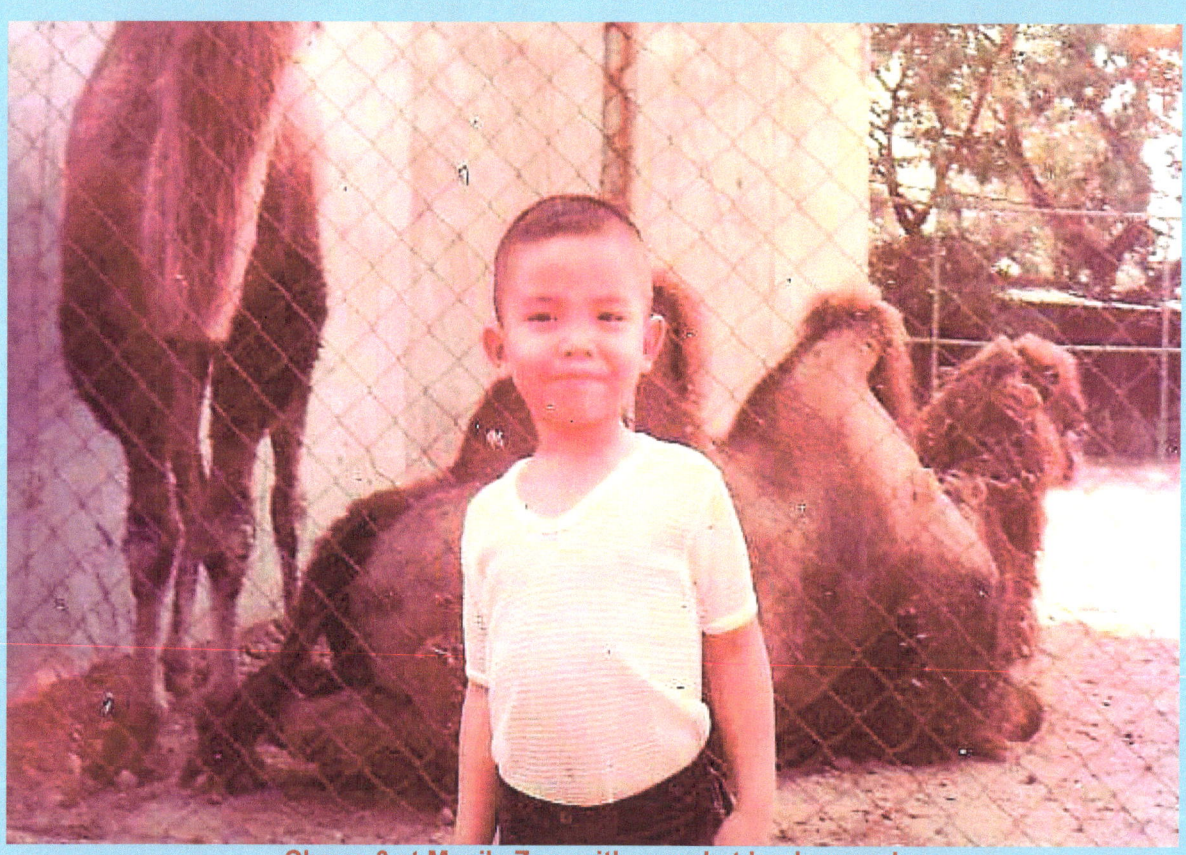

Chevy, 6 at Manila Zoo, with camel at background

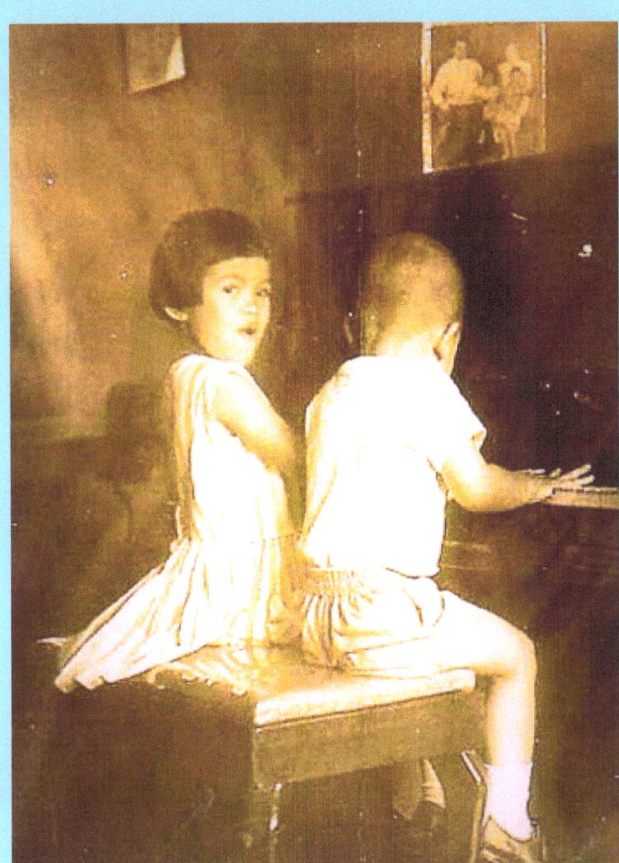 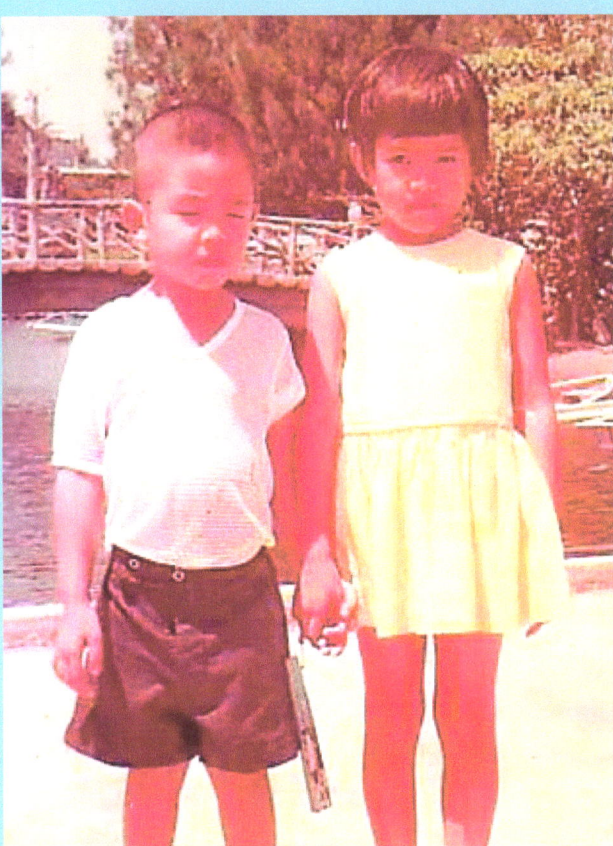

Young Techie and Chevy at piano . . . . + Chevy and Techie at Manila Zoo

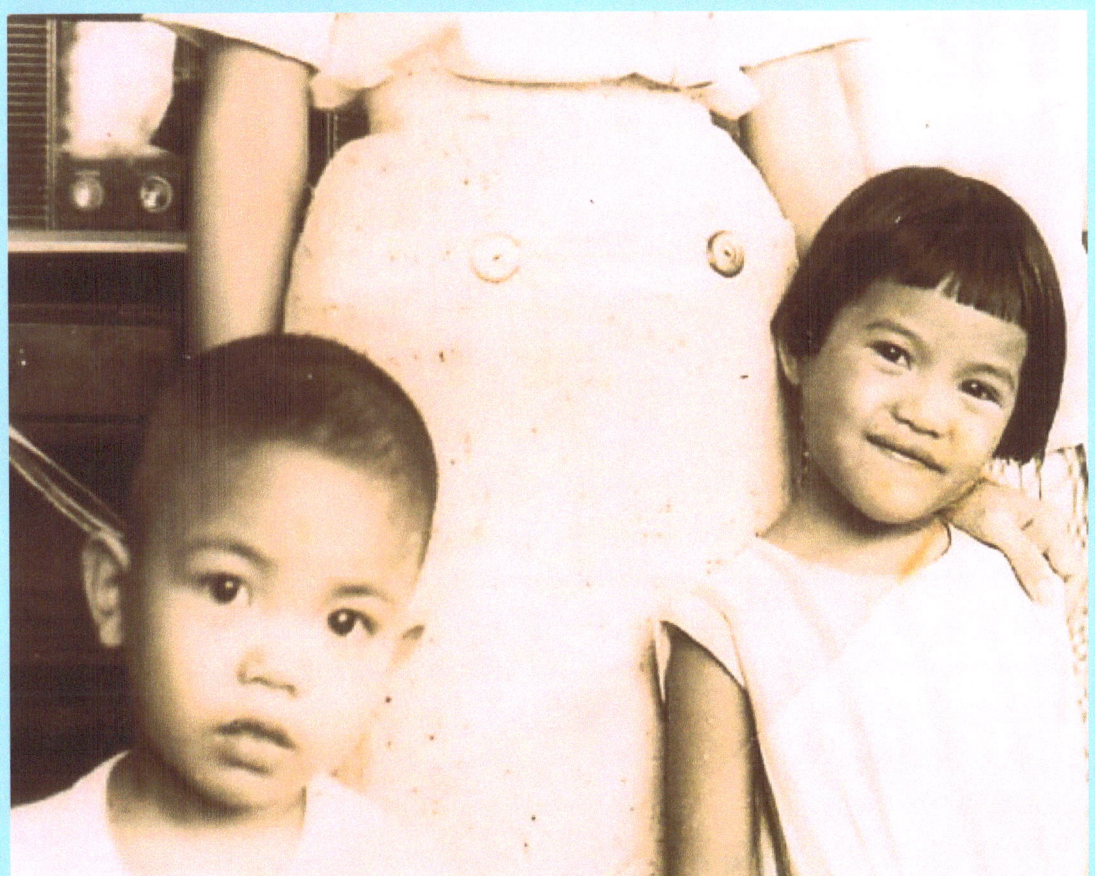

Chevy, 1 & Techie, 3

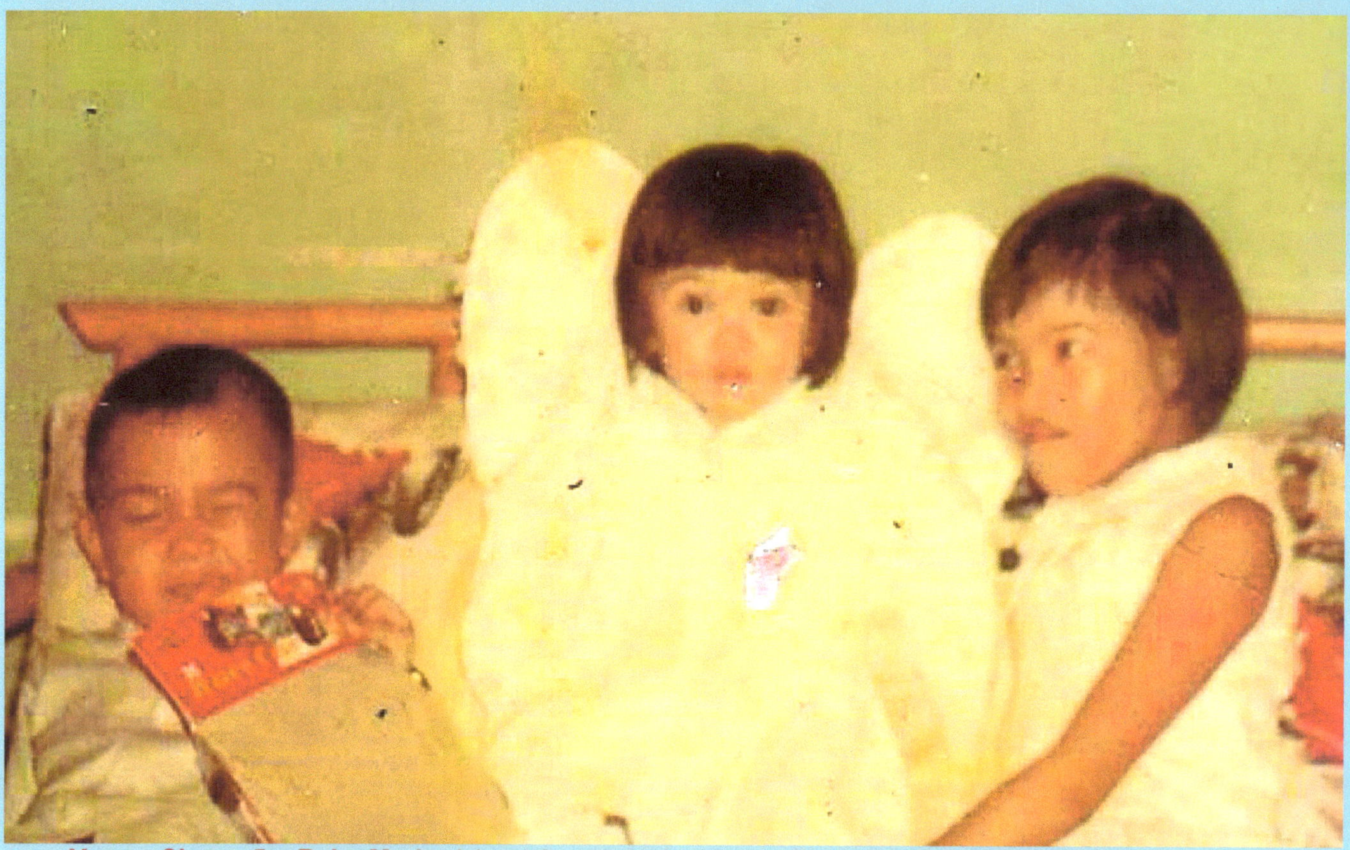

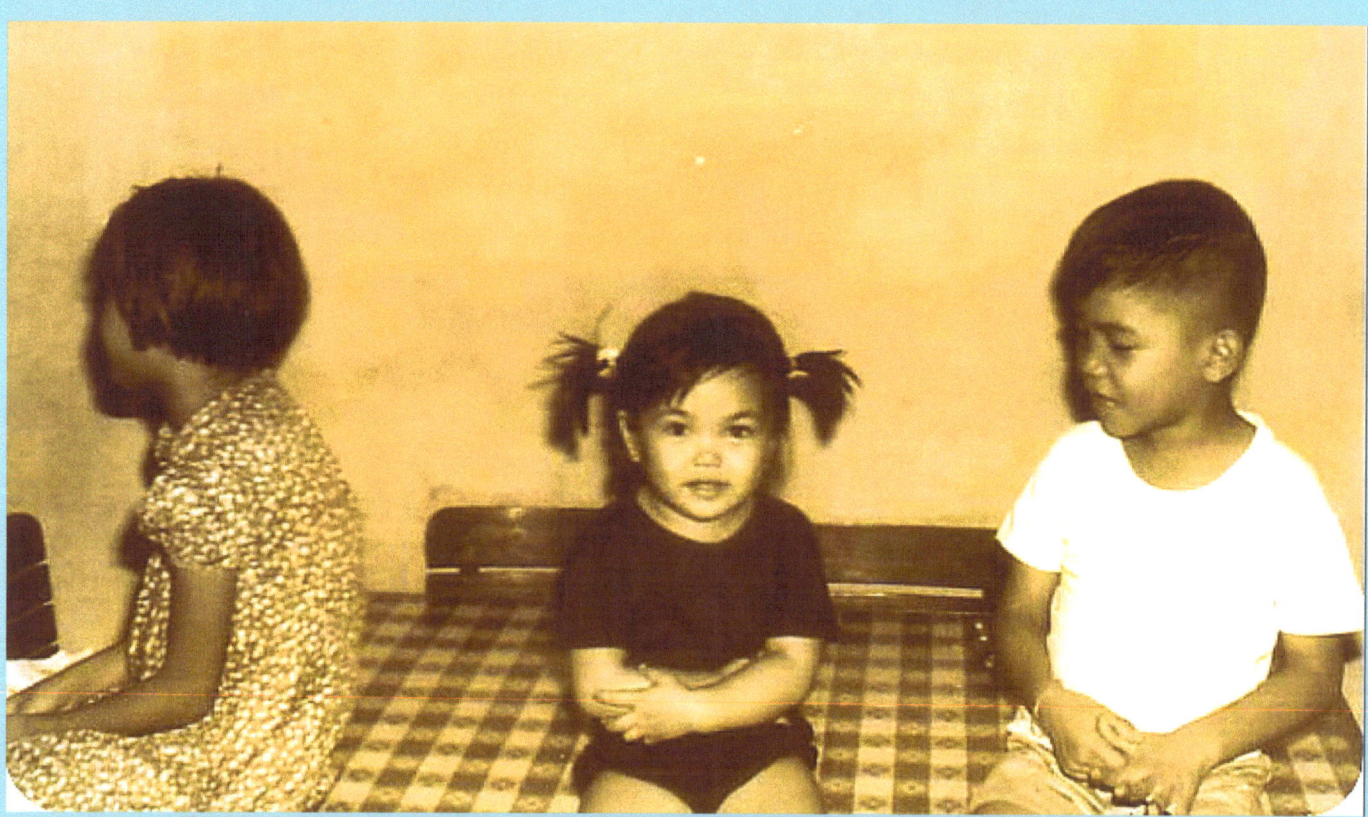

Young Chevy, 5 + Baby Marie, 1 (angel costume) + Young Techie, 7, at home in Malate Apartment

Techie,8, back to camera + Baby Marie,1, + Chevy,6, at home in Malate Apartment

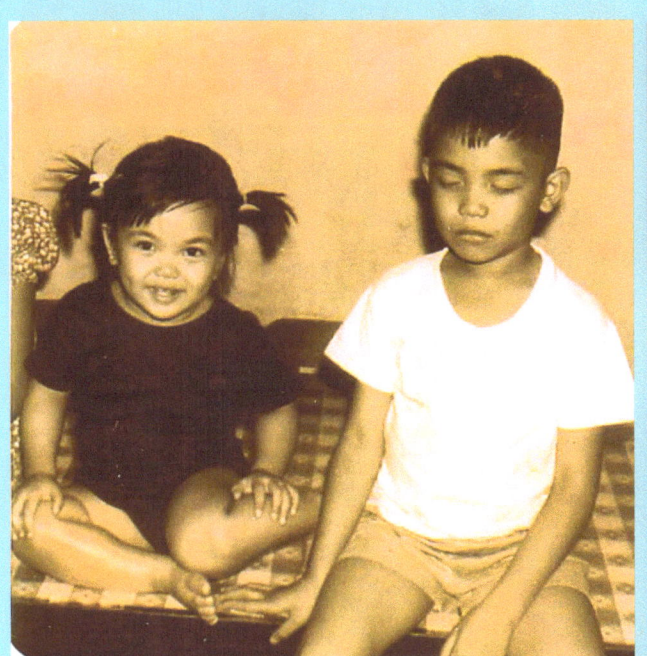
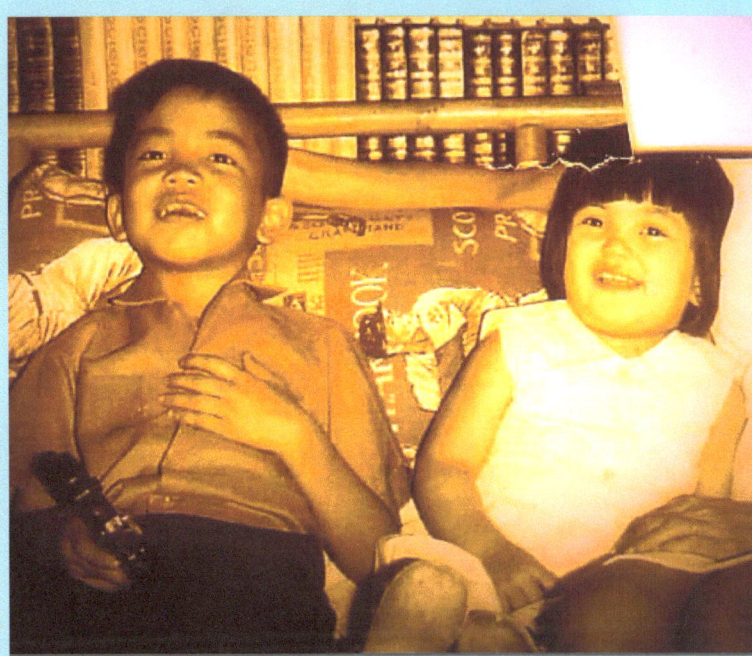

2 Pics: Baby Marie, 1 + Chevy, 6, at home in Malate Apartment

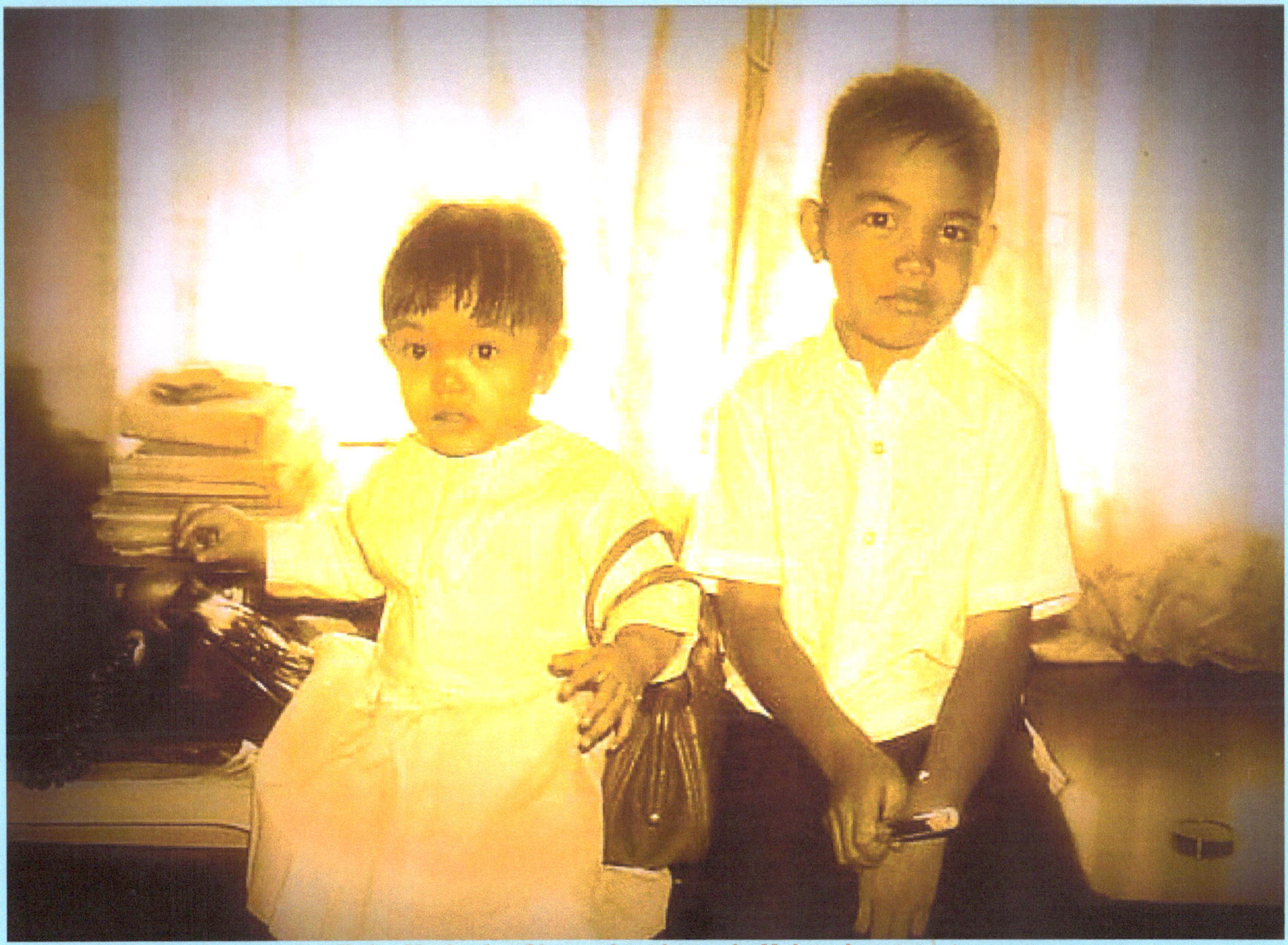

Baby Marie, 1 + Chevy, 6, at home in Malate Apartment

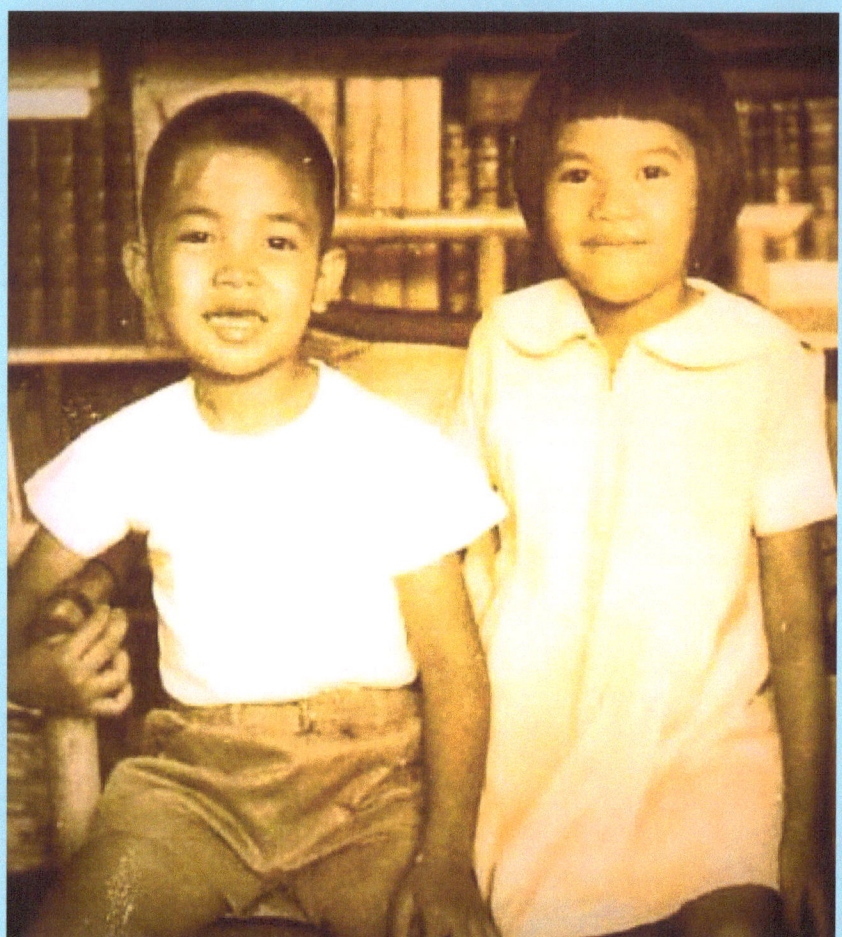 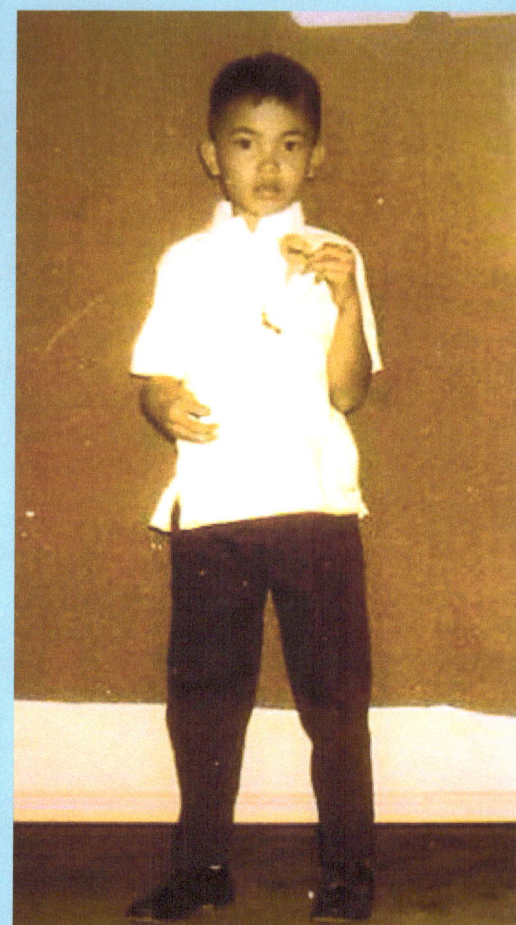

Chevy, 6 + Techie, 8, at home in Malate Apt. . . . . + + + Chevy, 7, in a school program

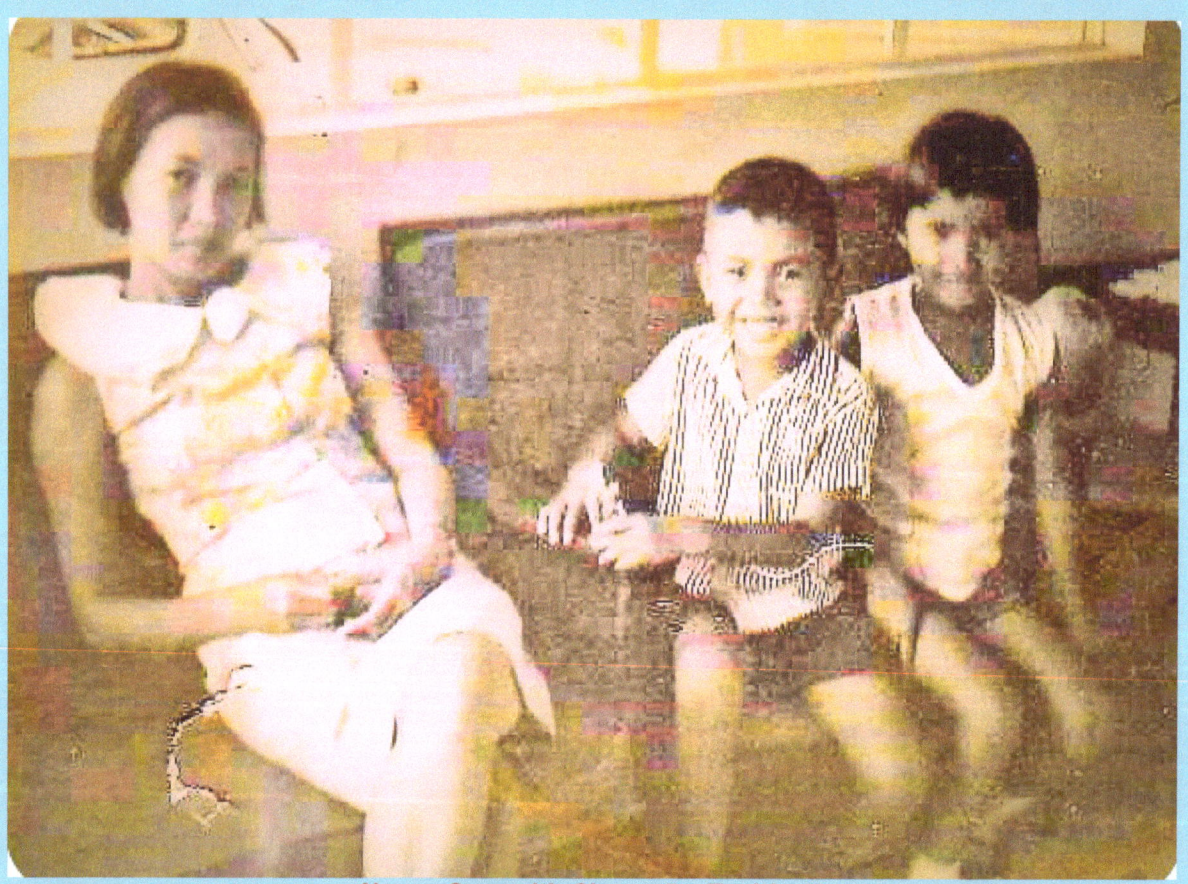

Nanay Cora with Chevy, 5 + Techie, 7

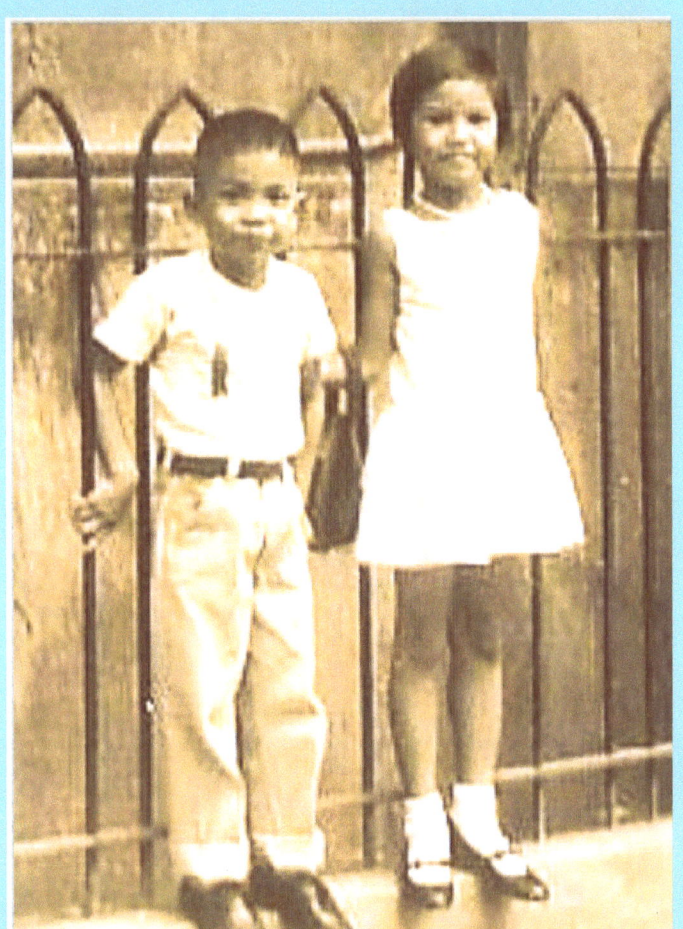
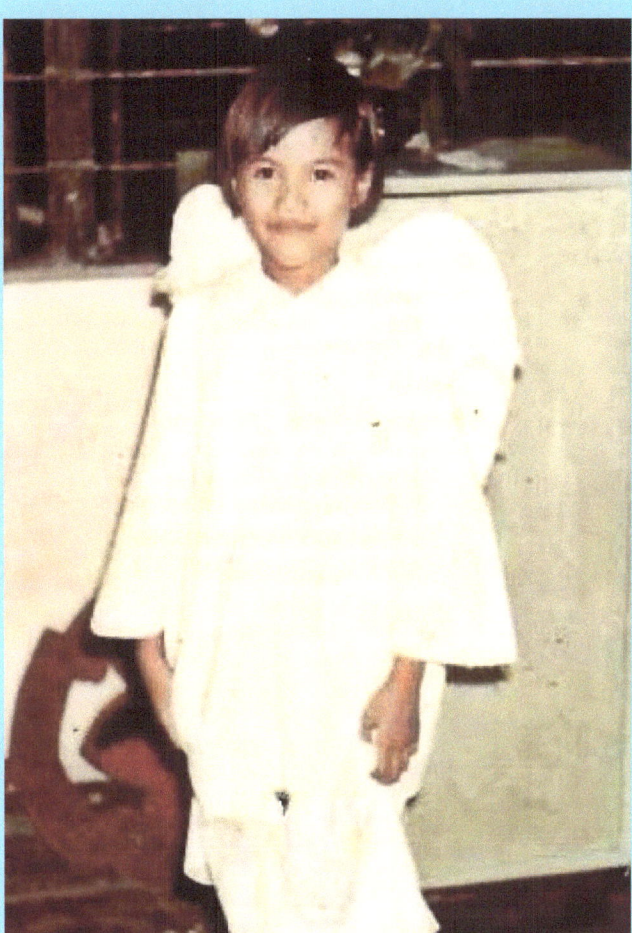

Chevy, 6 + Techie, 8, at Ellinwood Church . . . . + Techie, 10, in angel costume

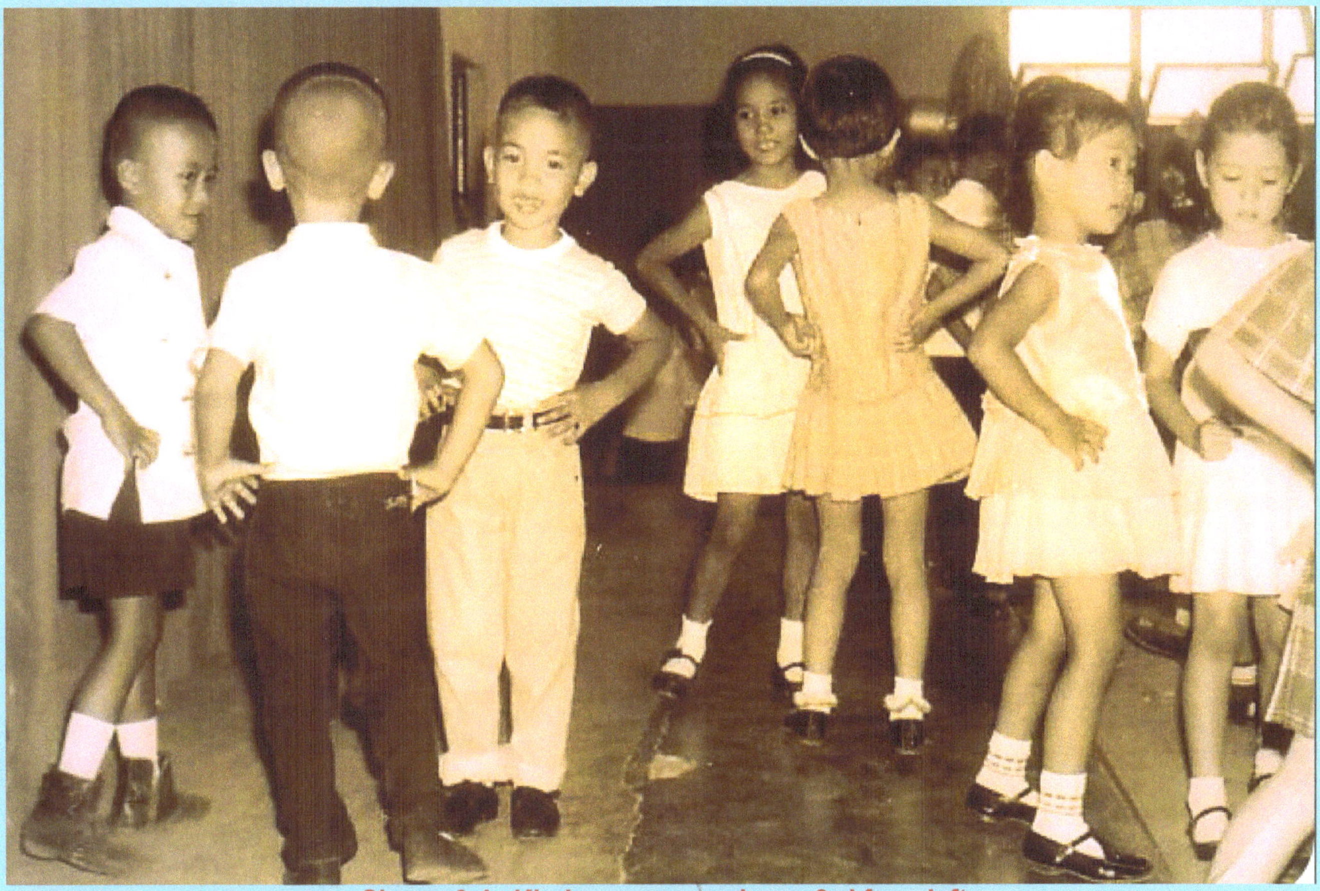

Chevy, 6, in Kinder program, shown 3rd from left

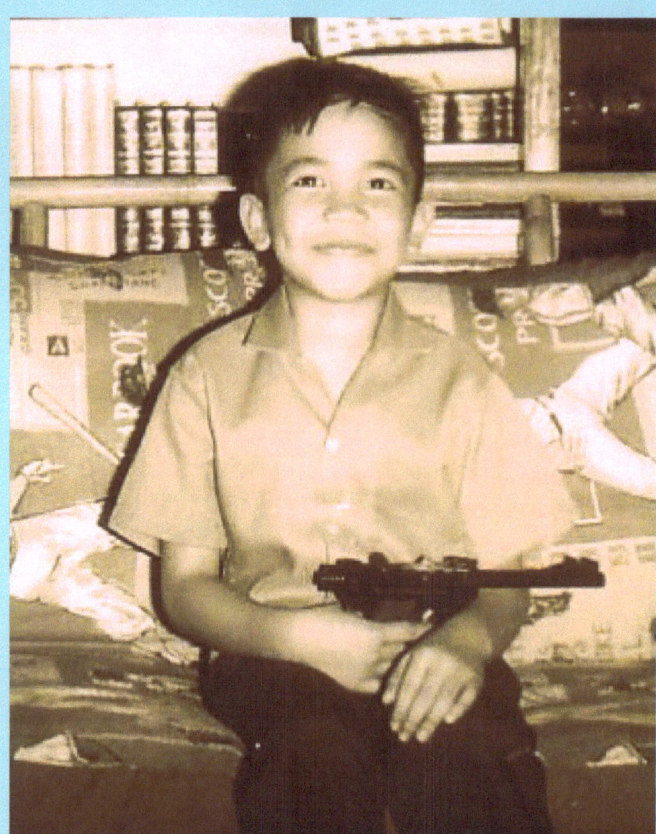 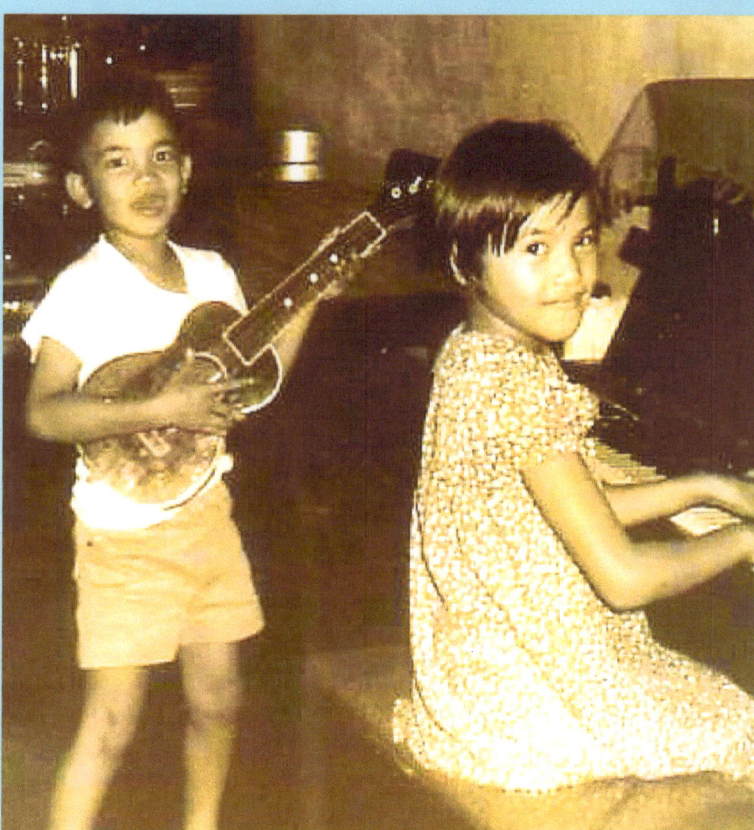

Chevy, 7, with a toy gun . . . . . + Chevy, 7 with uke + Techie, 9 at piano, at Malate Apartment home

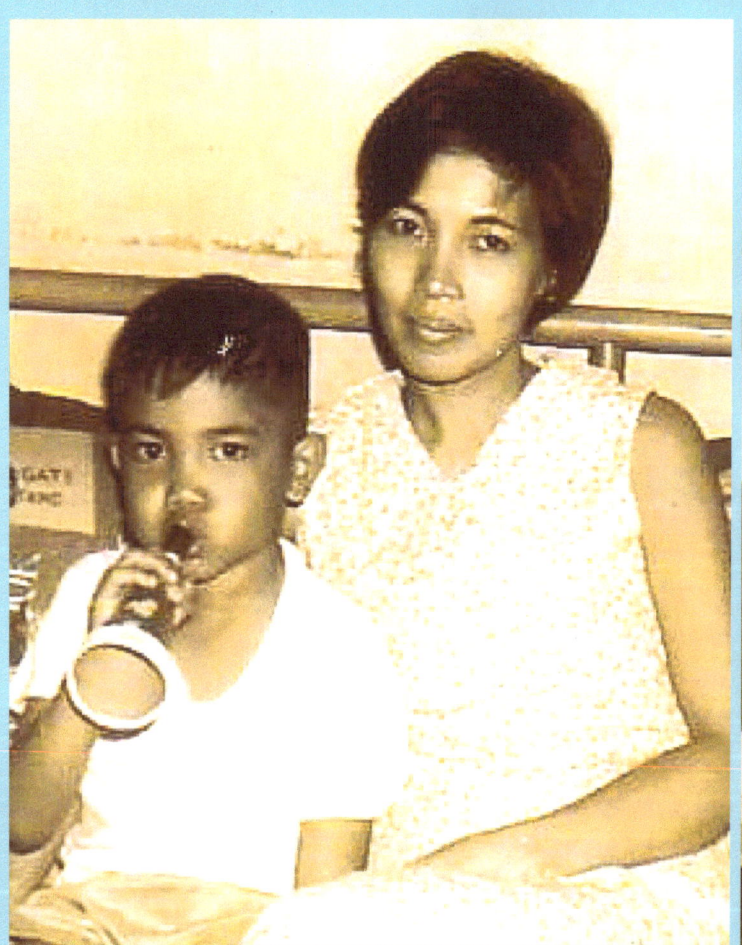 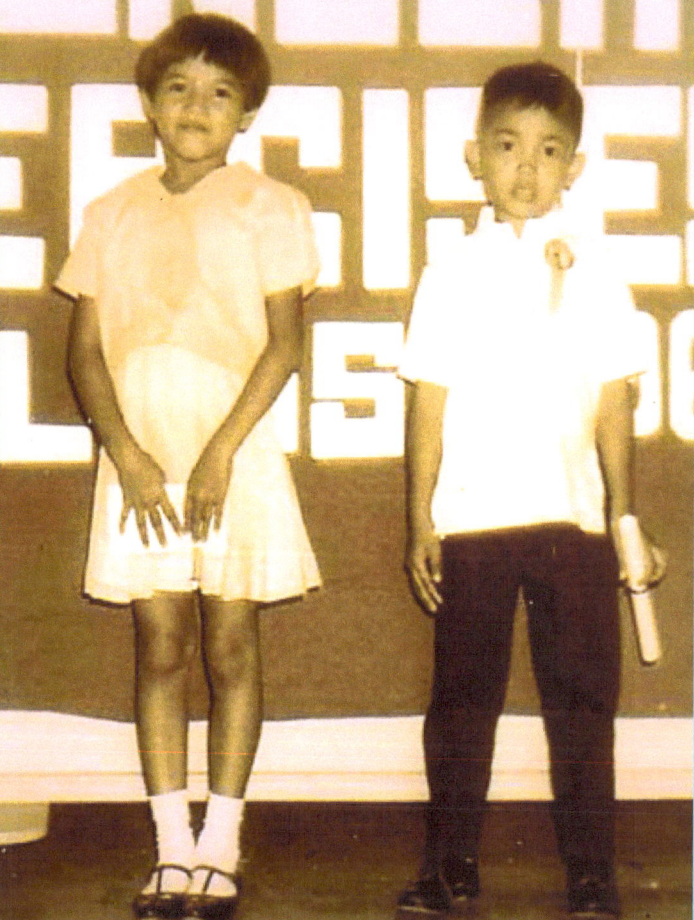

Chevy, 8 with Nanay Cora . . . . . + Techie, 9, + Chevy, 7, in a class program at PCCh Elem. School

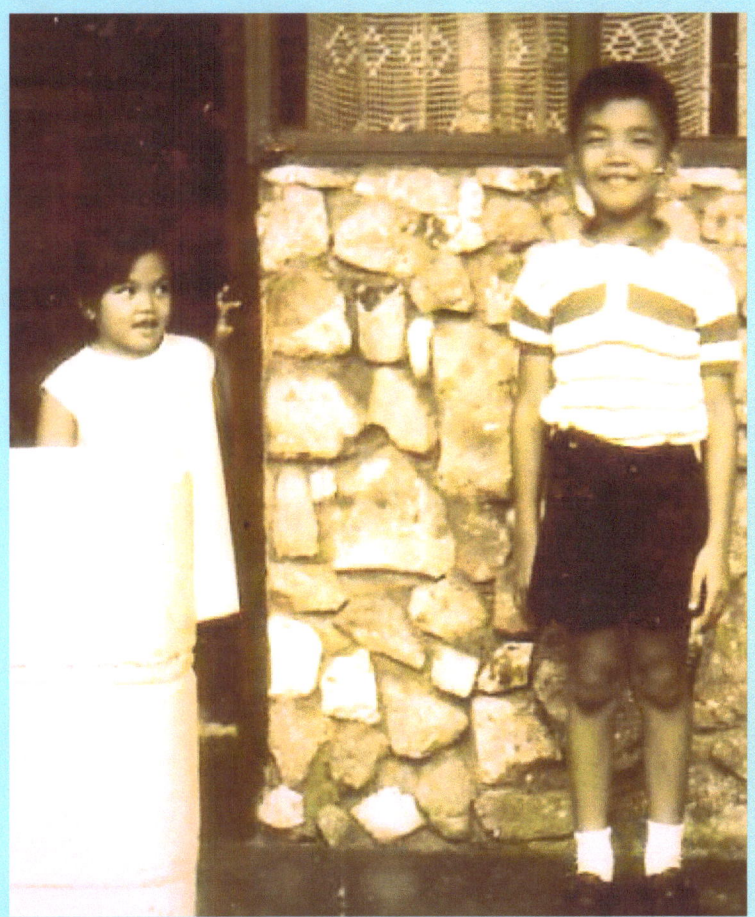
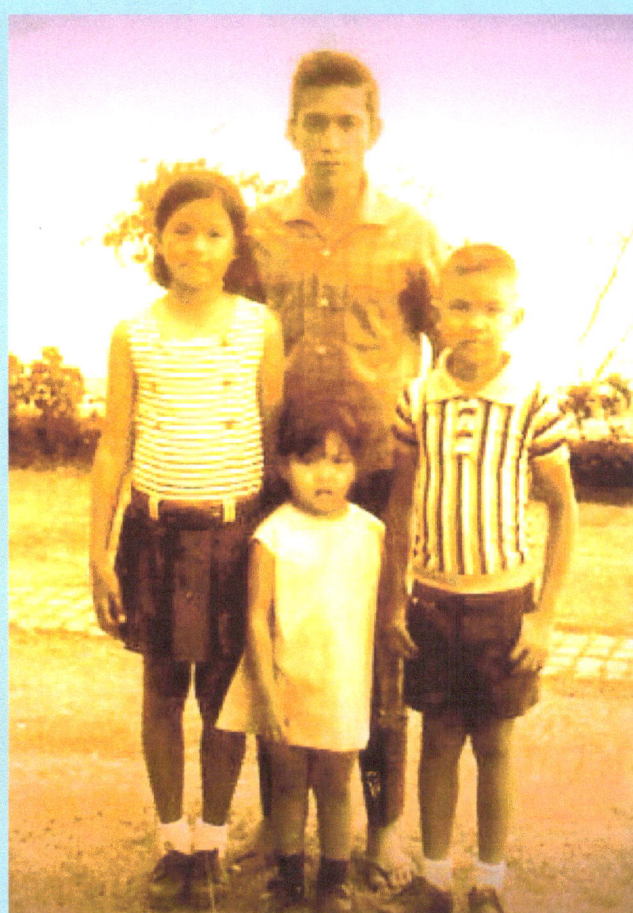

Marie, 3 + Chevy, 8, at Apartment in Malate . . . . . + Their Uncle Paquito + Techie,10 + Marie,3 + Chevy,8

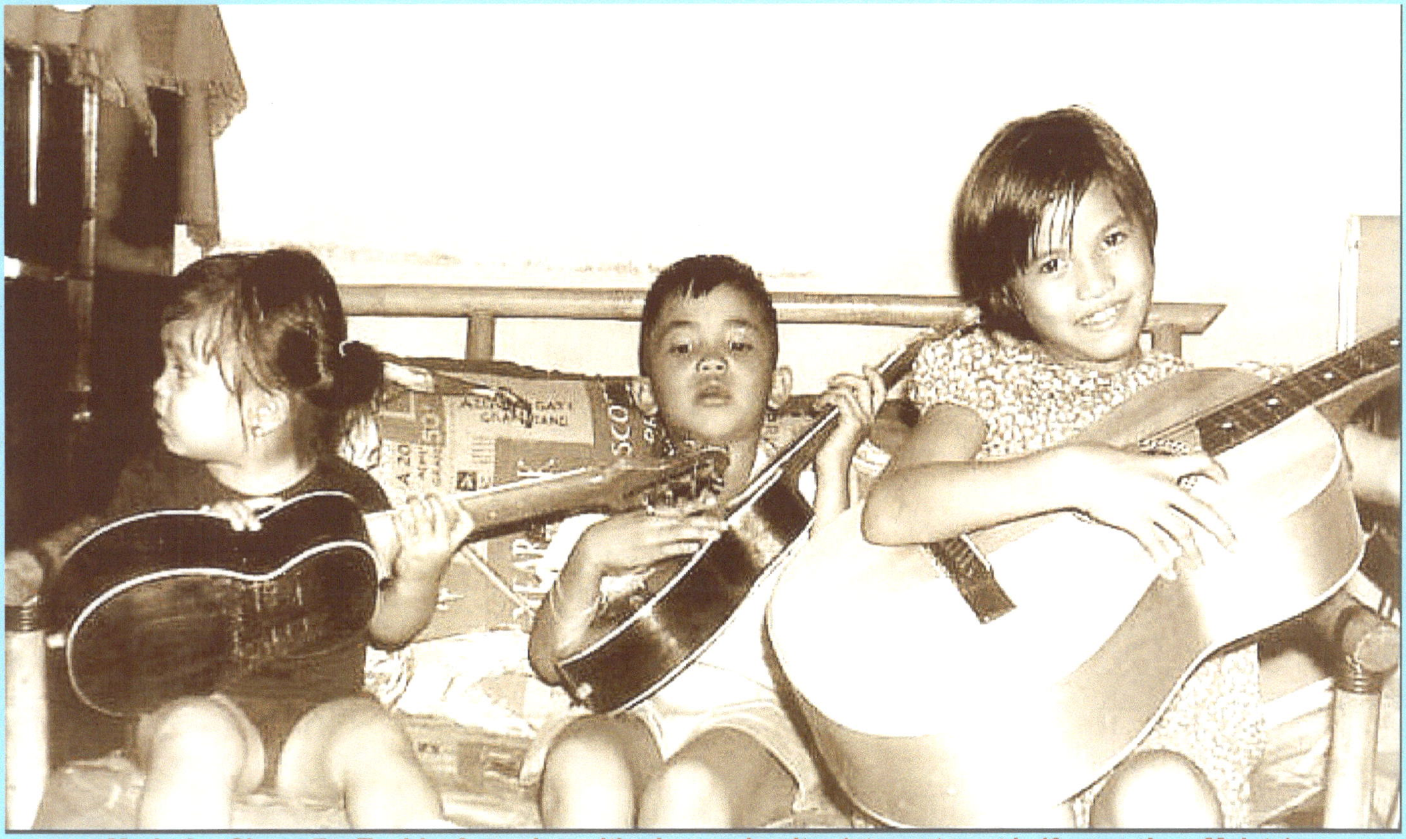

Marie,2 + Chevy,7 + Techie, 9, posing with ukes and guitar (at apartment in Kansas Ave, Malate)

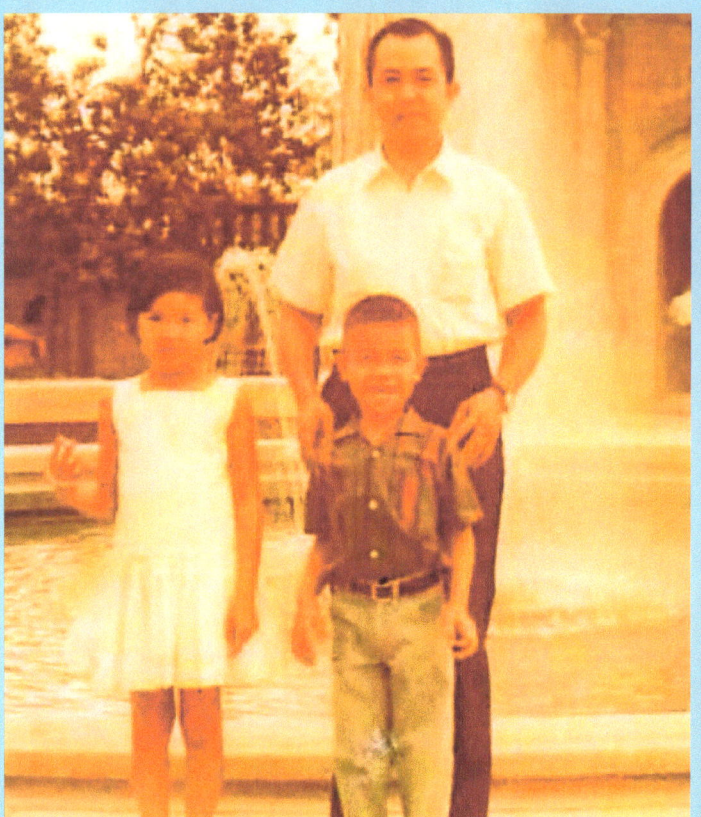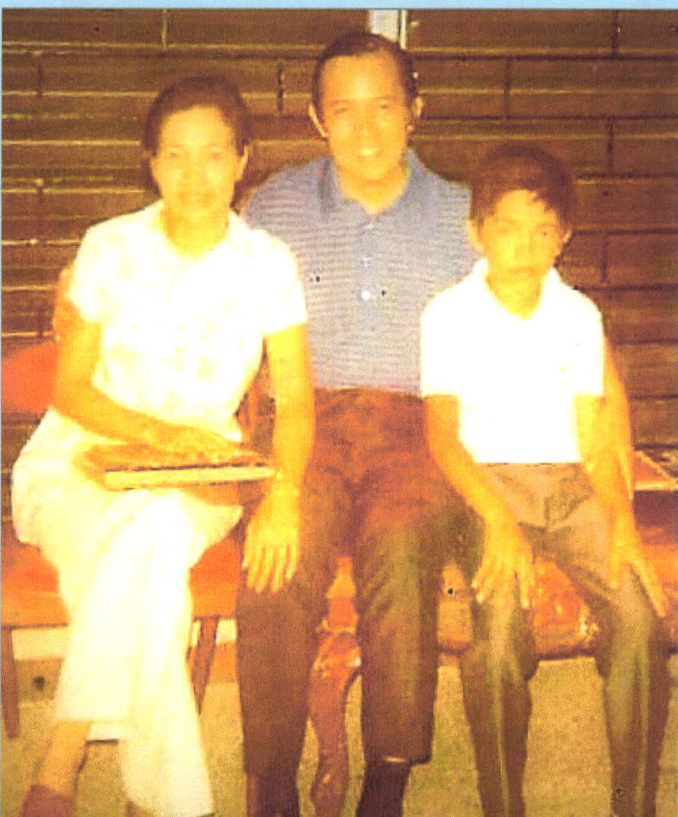

Techie, 8 + Chevy, 6, with Tatay Job . . . . . + Nanay Cora + Tatay Job with Chevy, 12

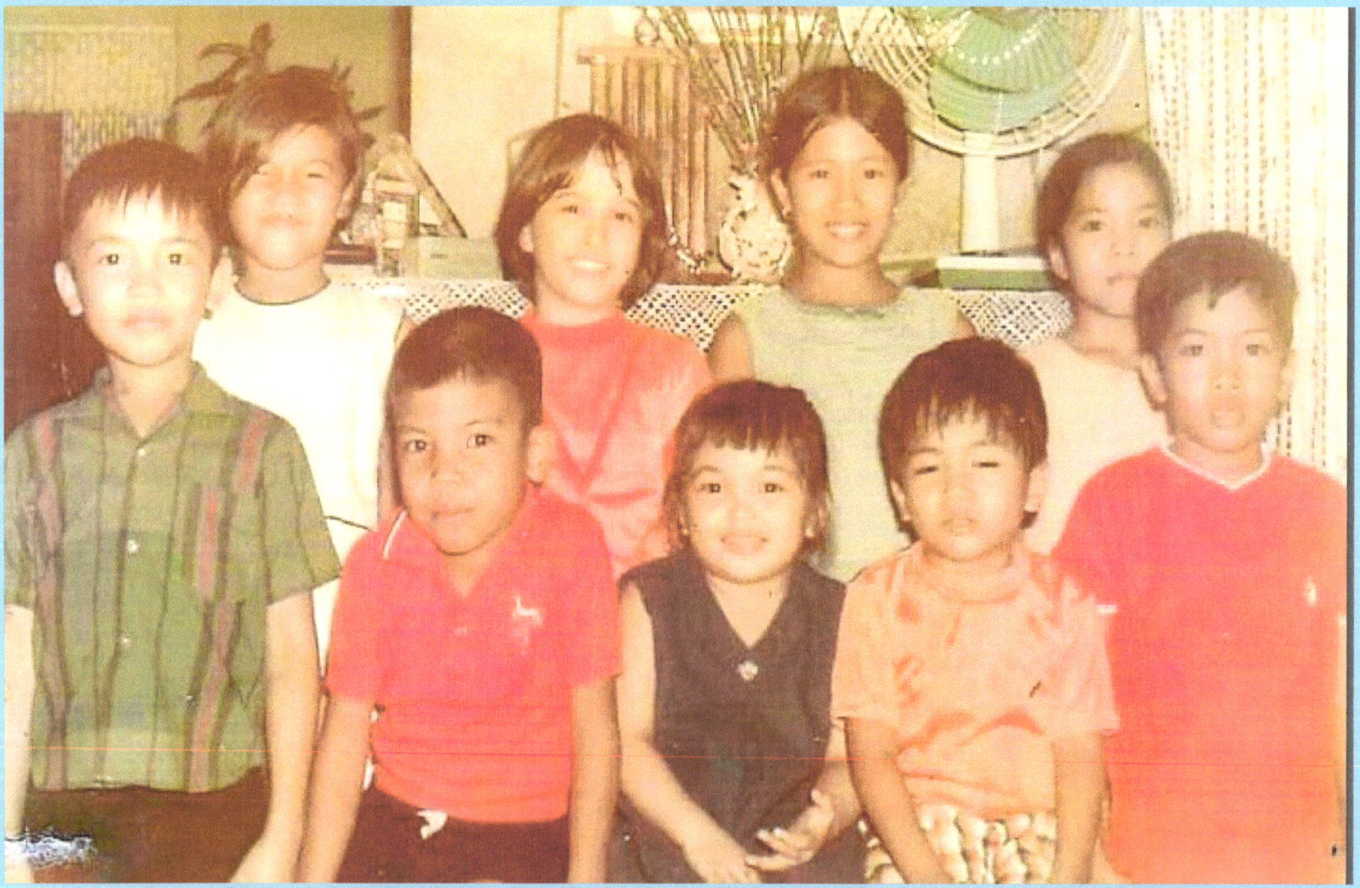

Front Row: Chevy Elizes,7 + Ferrer relative + Marie Elizes,3 + Roman Ferrer,3 + Leo Ferrer, 7 . . . . .
Back Row: Techie Elizes, 9 + Mimi Hollmann, 10 + Ana Grace Ferrer,11 + Cynthia Ferrer,10
(Group picture of young relatives)

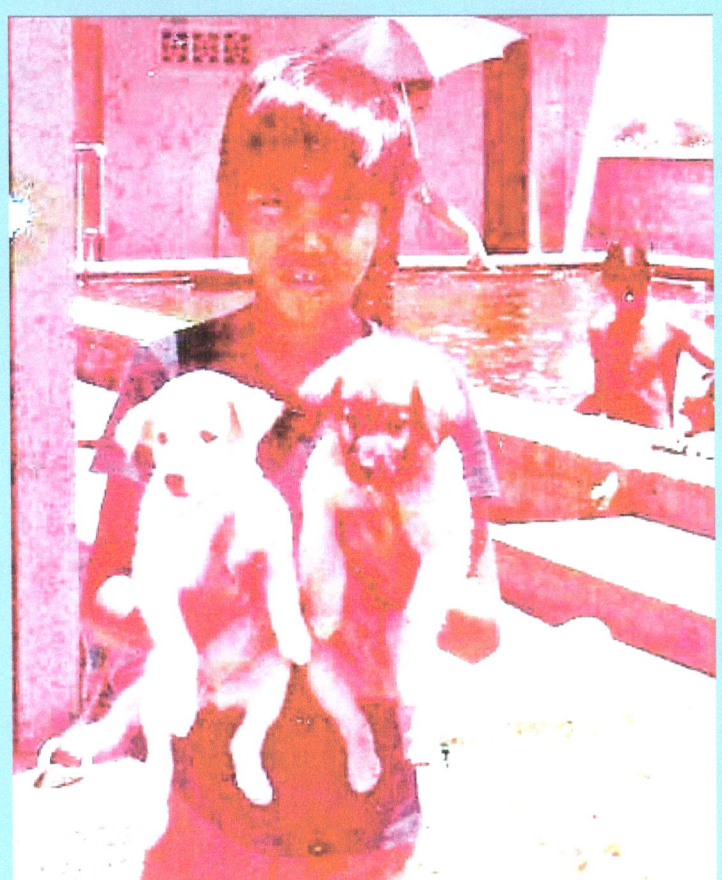
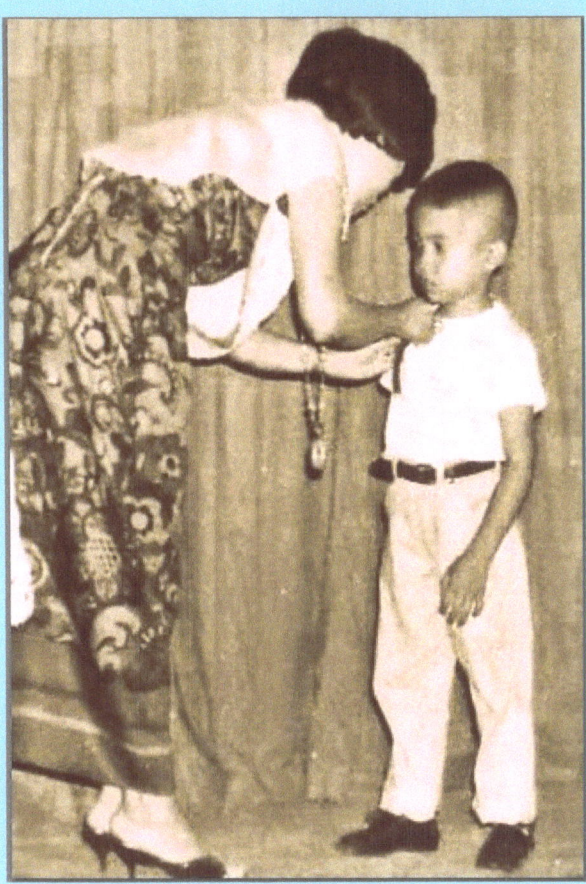

Chevy, 10 + his favorite pet dogs . . . . . + Teacher with Chevy,7, class program

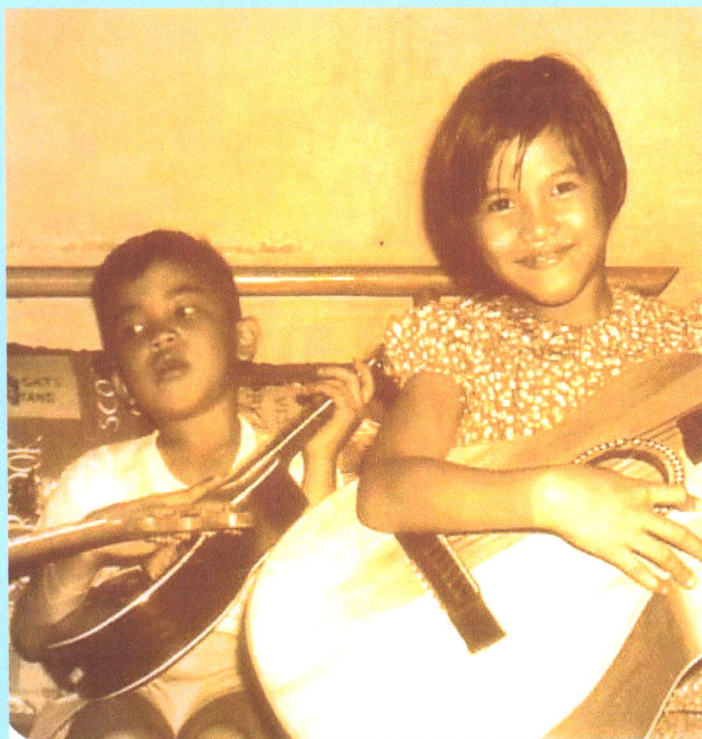
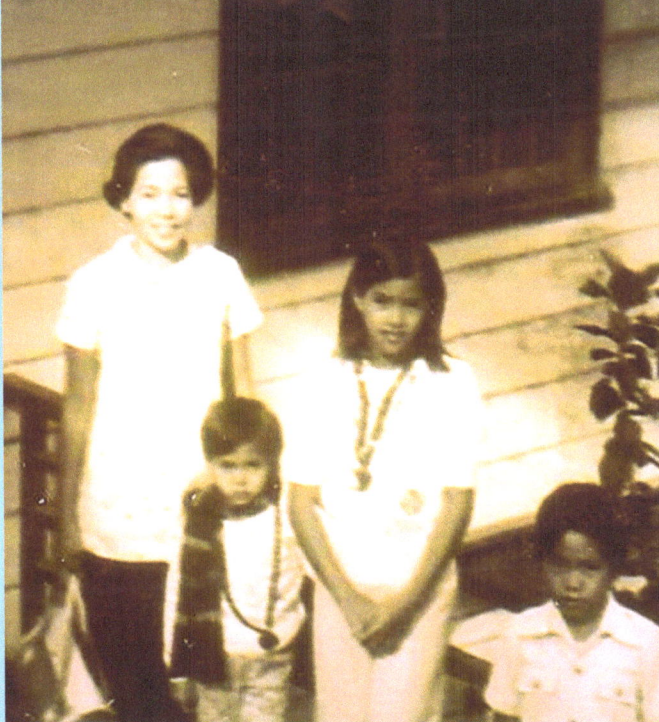

Chevy,6 with uke + Techie, 8 with guitar (posing) . . . . + Nay Cora with Marie,4 + Techie,11 + Chevy,9 (Baguio)

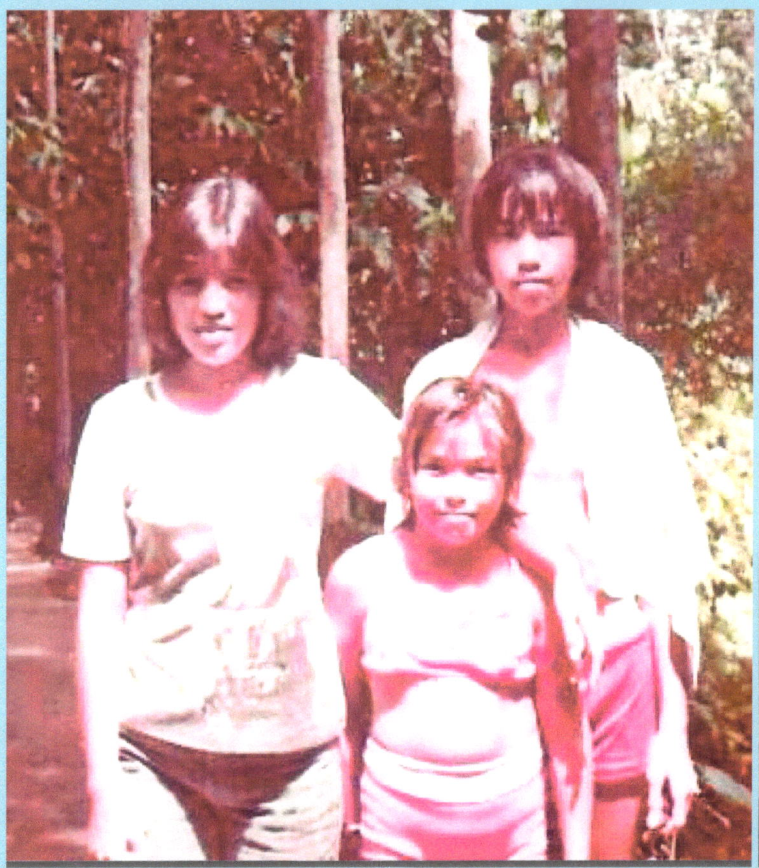

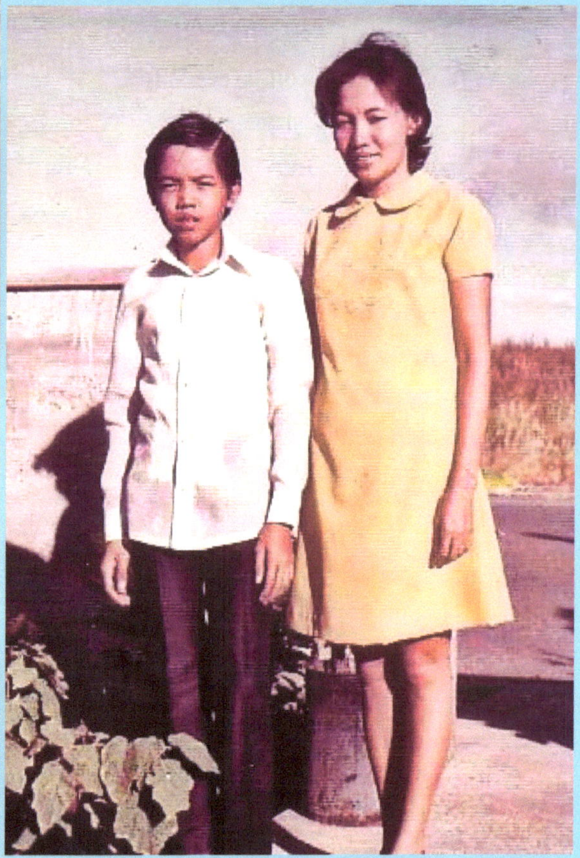

Techie, 17 + Marie, 10 + Chevy, 15 (Baguio Trip). . . . . Chevy, 13 + Nanay Cora

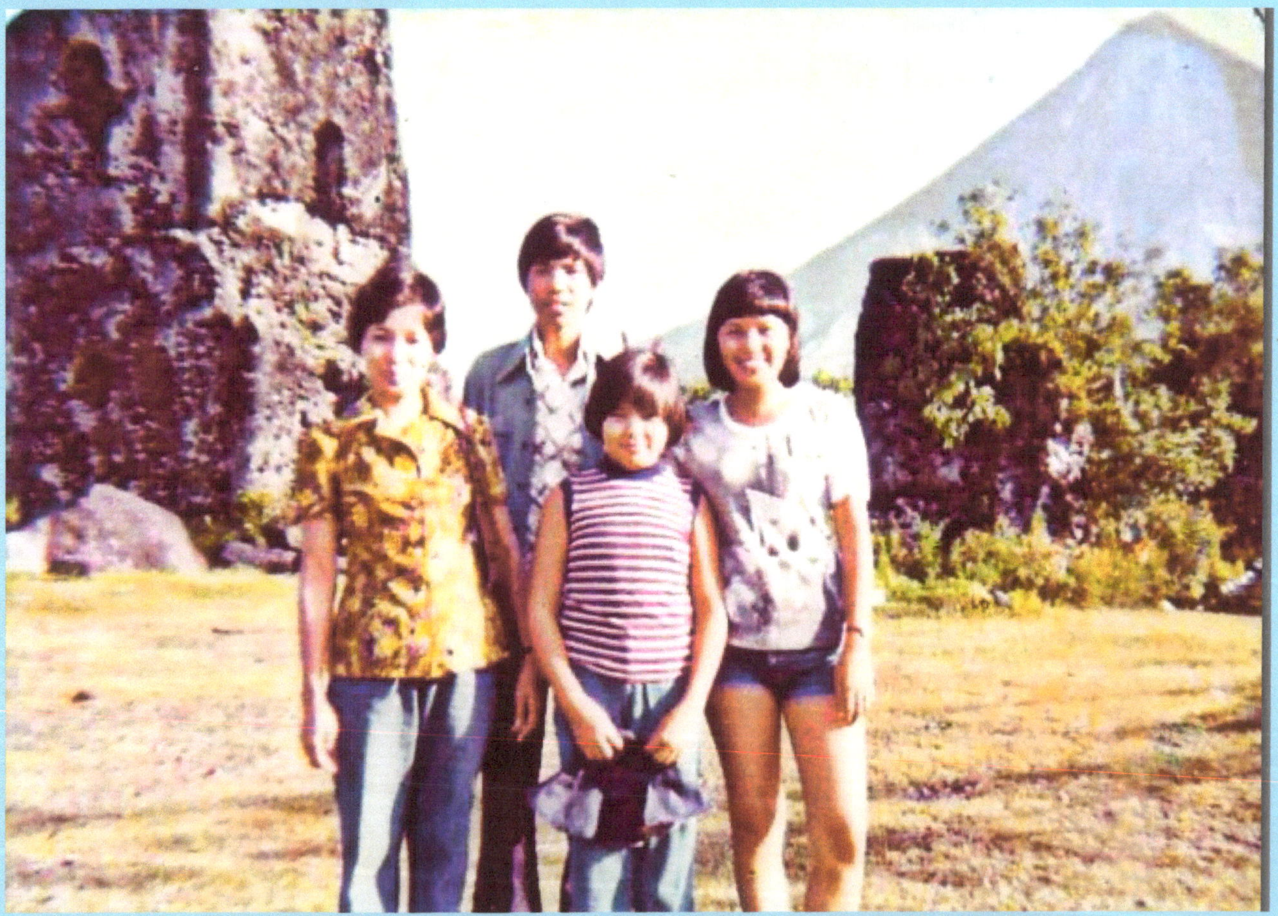

1978 Trip to Bicol: L-R: Nanay Cora + Chevy, 16 + Marie,10 + Techie,18

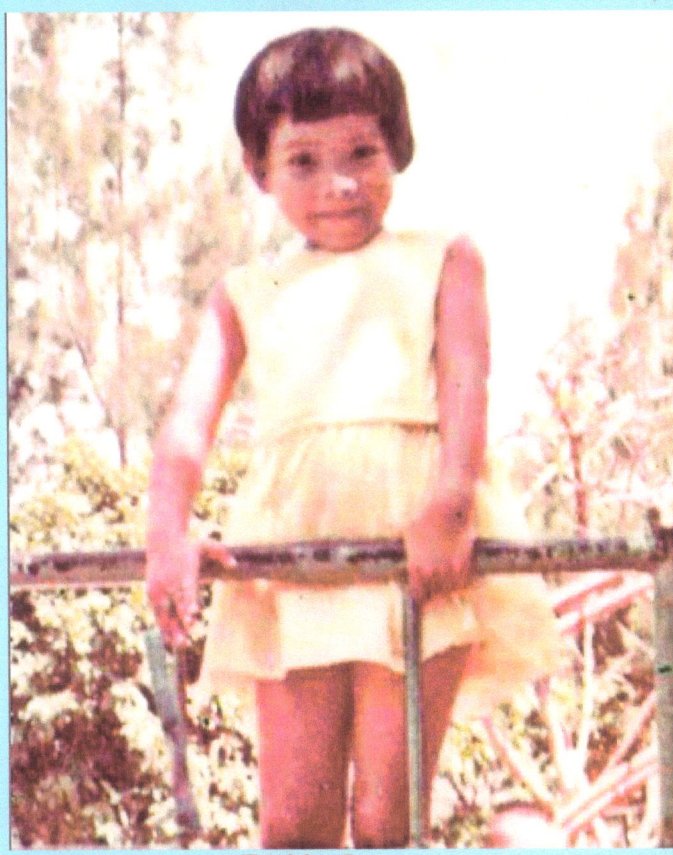

Techie, 5

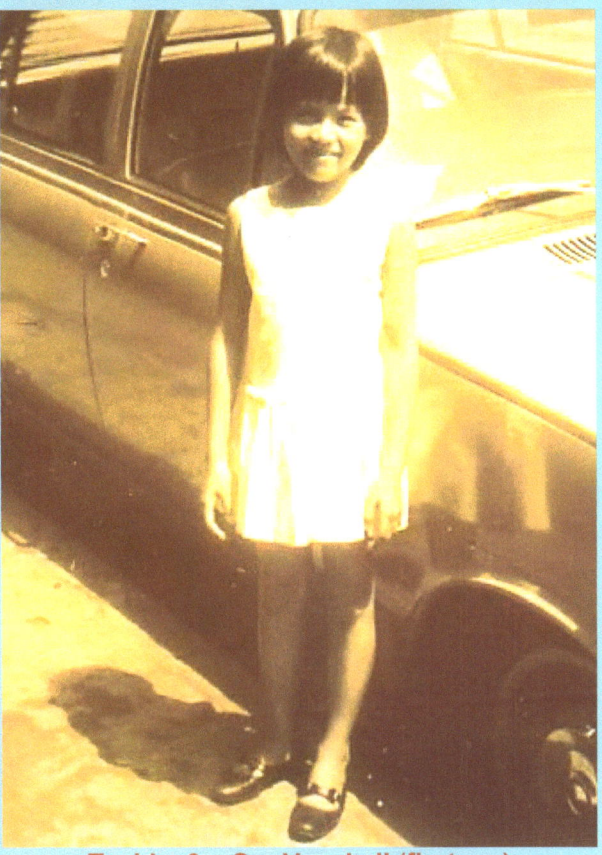

Techie, 6 + Our Vauxhall (first car)

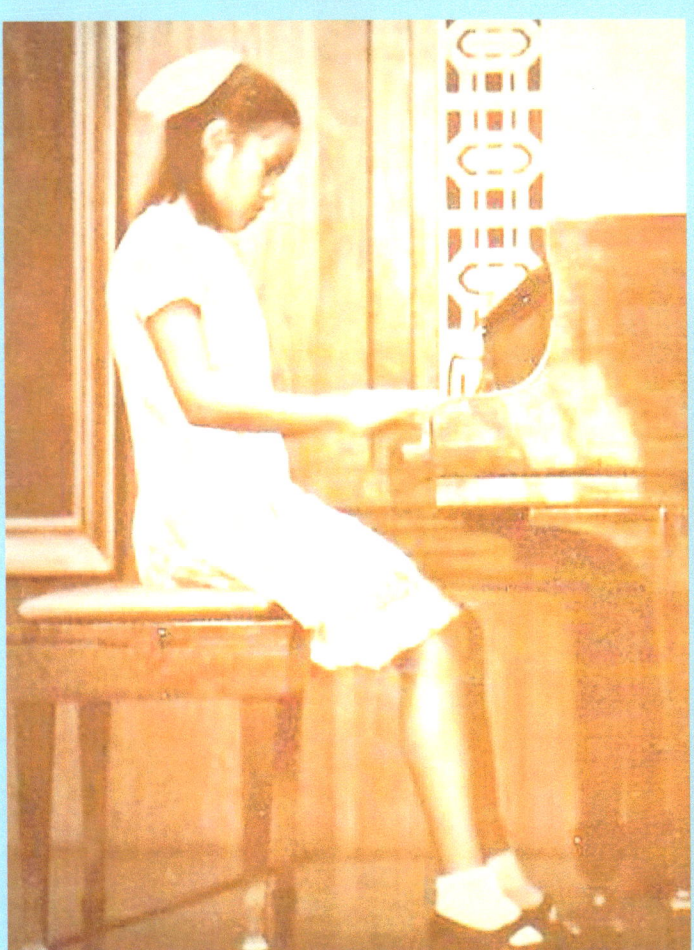

Techie, 11, Piano Recital. . .

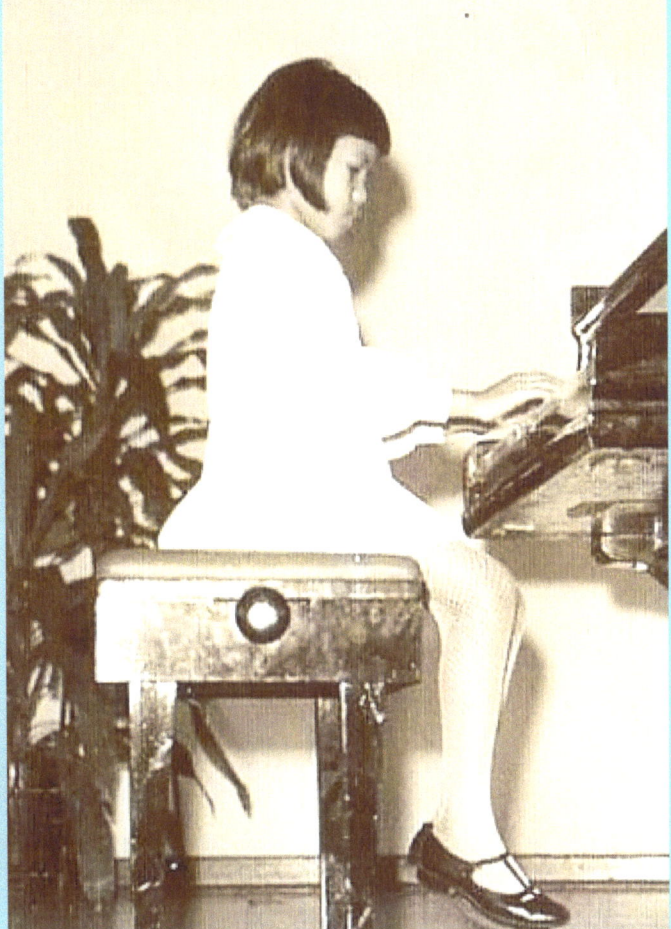

. . Techie, 8, Piano Recital

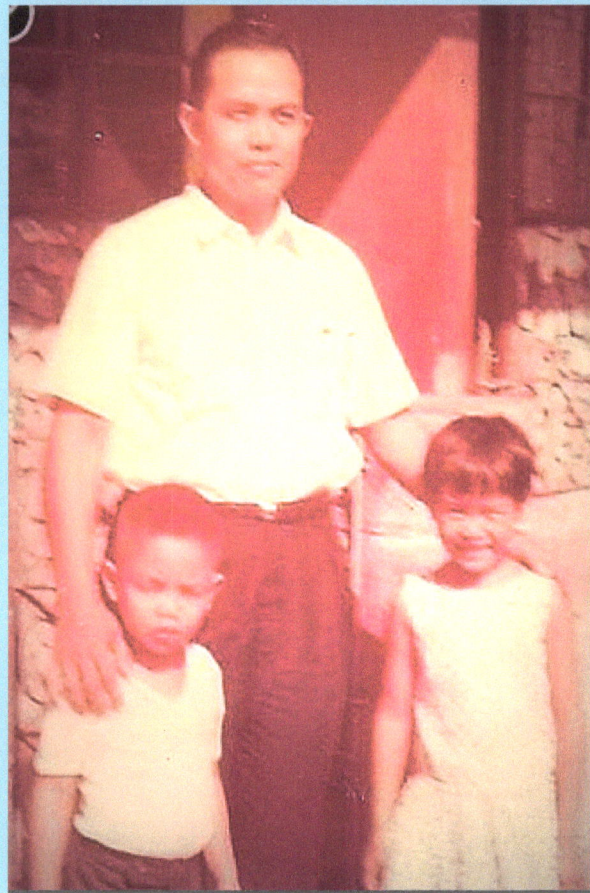

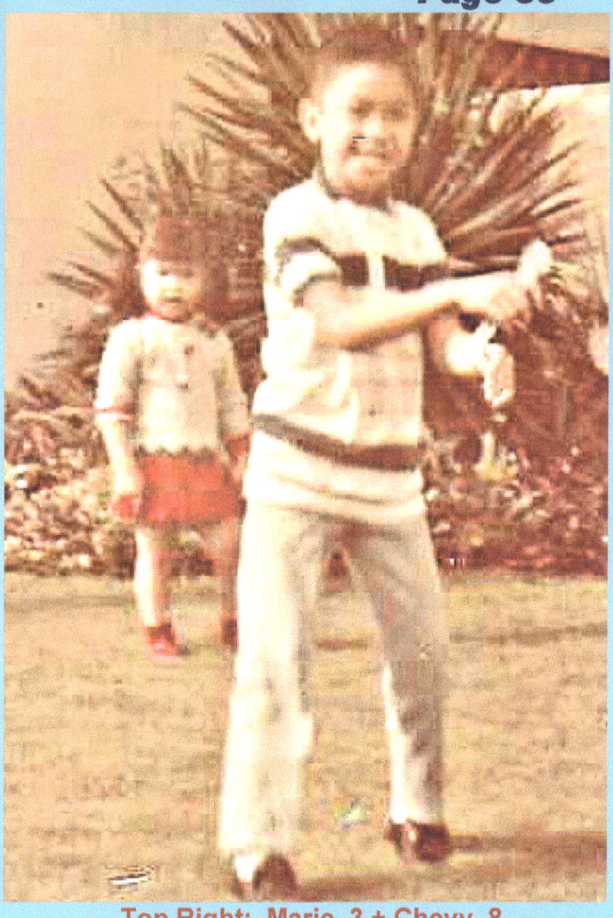

Tatay Job + Chevy, 3 + Techie, 5 . .   . . . Top Right: Marie, 3 + Chevy, 8

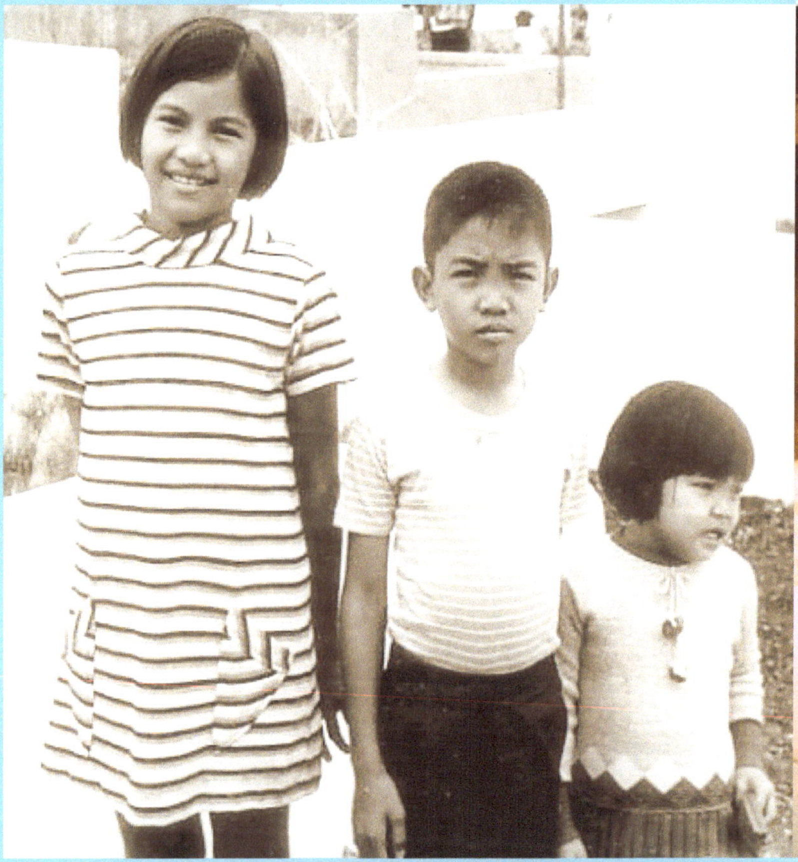

Techie,11 + Chevy, 9 + Marie, 4 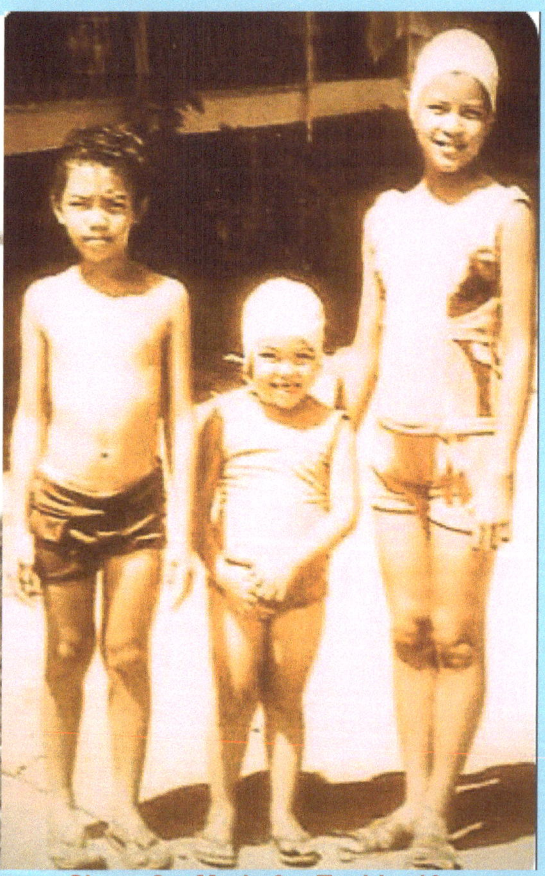 . . .   Chevy,8 + Marie,3 + Techie, 10

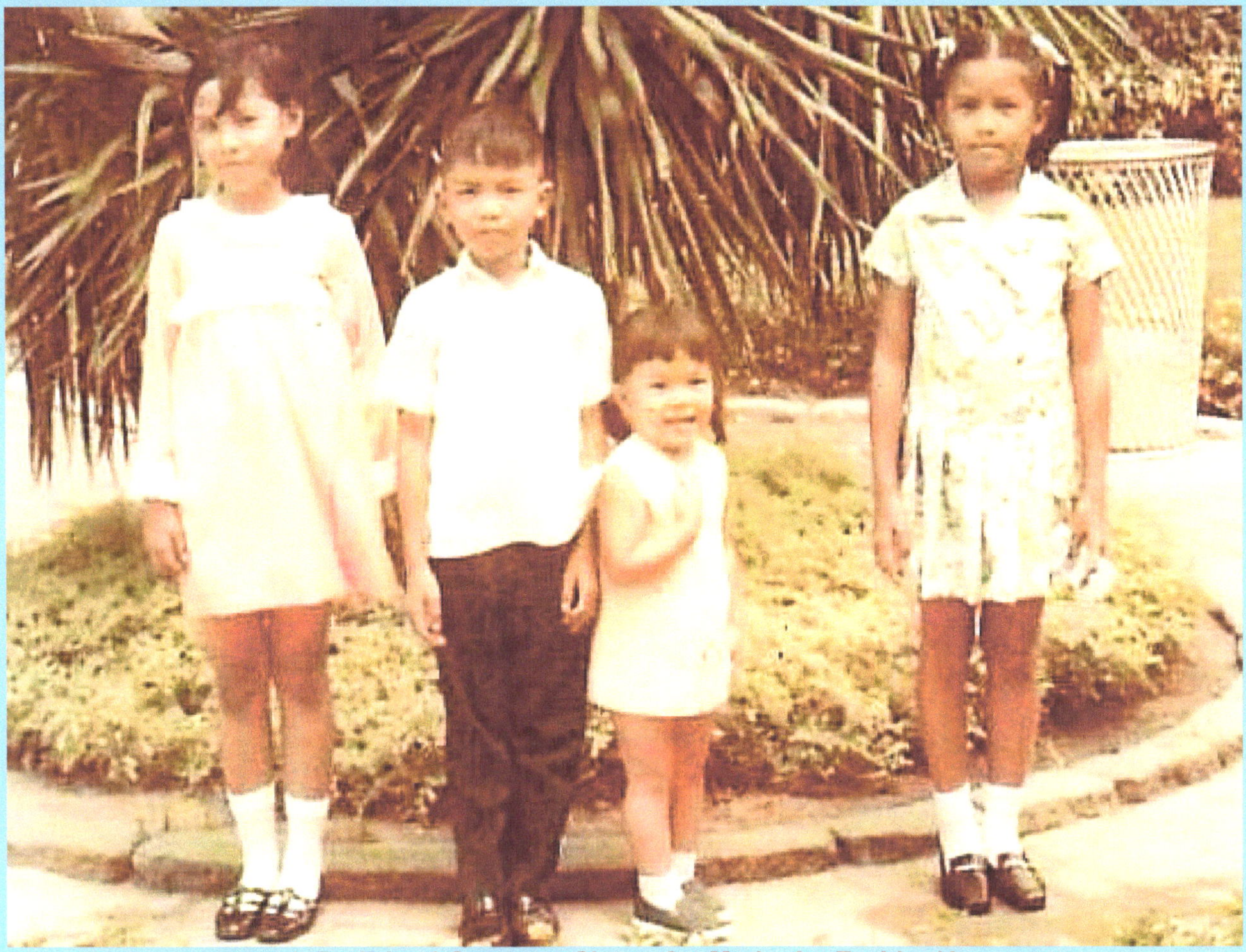

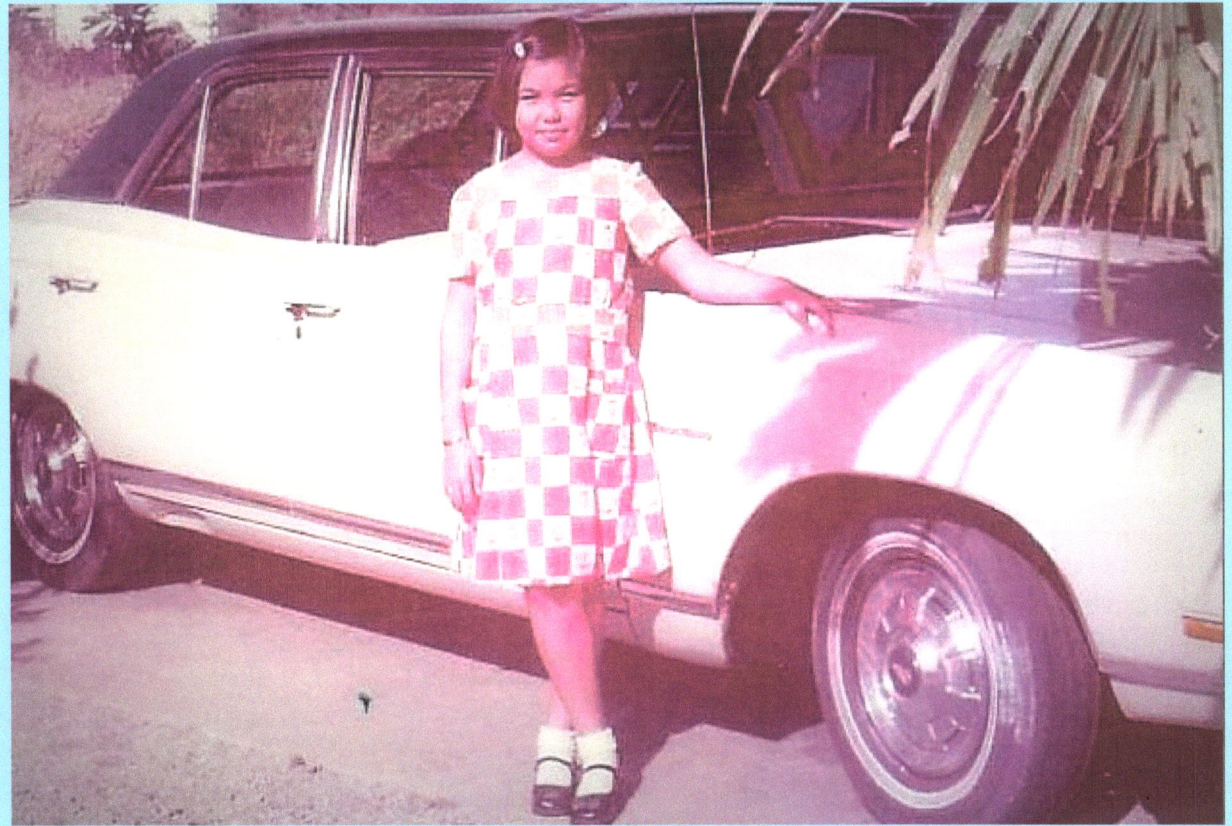

L-R: Friend Gemma + Chevy, 8 + Marie, 3 + Techie, 10

Marie, 10 + our Plymouth

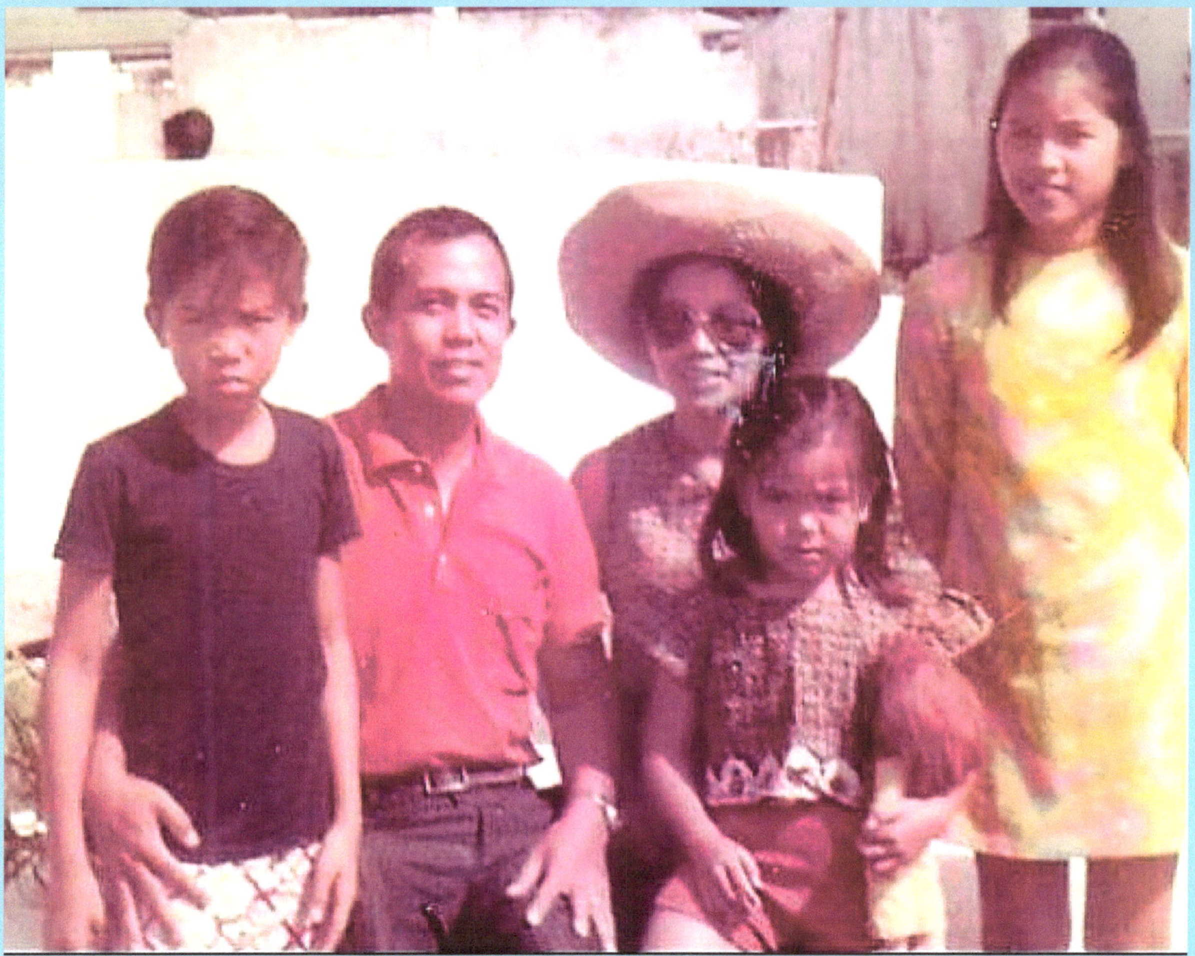

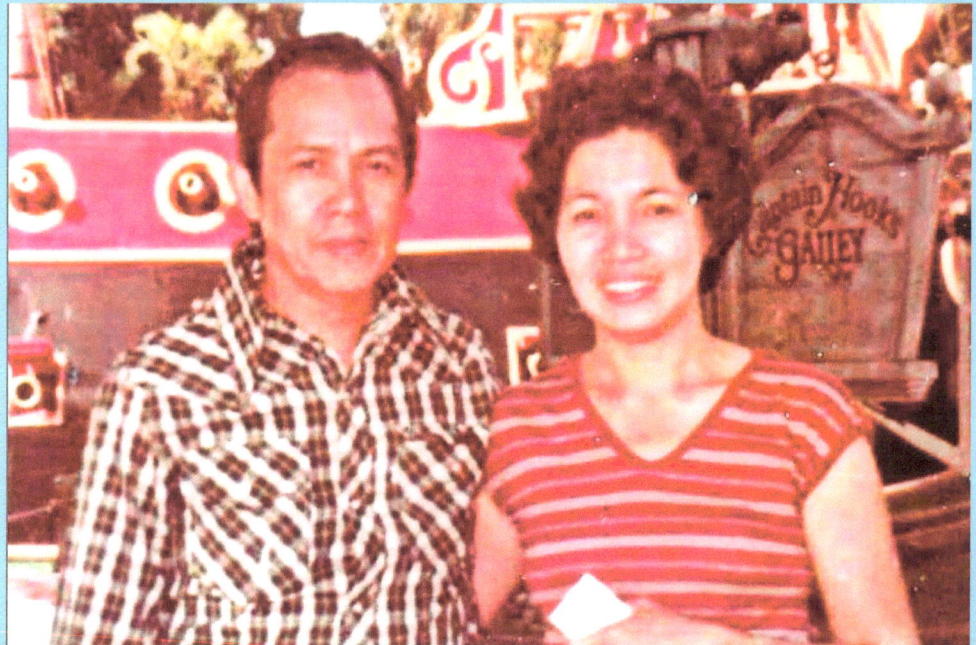

L-R: Chevy,12+ Tatay Job + Nanay Cora + Marie, 6 + Techie, 14

Many thanks for viewing our Pics Part 1. We published this book showing our younger years and eventual wedding and our 3 children during their formative years. This is about years 1950s and 1960s.
Published by Tatay Jobo Elizes in 2014 and printed in USA under these ISBN Codes:
ISBN - 13: 978 - 1503326767   and   ISBN - 10: 1503326764
Available at websites: http://tinyurl.com/mj76ccq + www.jobelizes.webs.com + www.tatayjobo.com
Contact emails: job_elizes@yahoo.com + tatay@usa.com
"Gift yourself or somebody in paperback book or kindle"

www.ingramcontent.com/pod-product-compliance
Lightning Source LLC
Chambersburg PA
CBHW050356180526

45159CB00005B/2038